Found Herself

shell.chelle

Found Herself
shell.chelle

Copyright © 2024 shell.chelle
Found Herself

ISBN: 979-8-9912545-1-9

Book & Cover Design: Integrative Ink
www.integrativeink.com

Poetry about a girl.
Just a girl,
Living her life.
Writing down her dreams.
Just a girl.
Imperfect and flawed.
Found her love,
Inside of herself.
Writing some words.
Words that became poetry.

These words became a story.
Her Story.
A story of a girl who:

Lost Herself

Found Herself

Then learned to...

Love Herself

This little side note:

This is her experience.
Her point of view.
Her feelings.
Her perspective.
Her story of letting go.
Her story of leaving,
A world of black and white.
Leaving the darkness,
And finding her light.
Her story of arriving,
To where the grey area resides.
This place of surrender.
This place of light.
A story of her memory.
A story of her truth.
A story from her eyes.
A story from her heart.
A story from her mind.
A story that she remembers,
As she listened to herself.
As she listened on her path.
Her path to self-love.
Her path to self-worth.
Her path to authenticity.
Her path to alignment.
Her path to her soul.
Her path.
Her love.
This is her story.

Also, this.
(In very fine print.)

These words.
These are just words.
Words of poetry.
Poetry to read.
These are just words.
Beautiful words.
Words of poetry.

Found Herself

Found Herself

She found herself,
Inside of her pain.
Through this pain.
Feeling this pain.
She found herself.
She found her soul.
She found herself,
As she dealt with it all.
She found herself,
On this journey.
On this journey,
Of feeling her pain.
Dropping the illusion.
Dropping the façade.
Dropping her mask.
Her mask that she wore.
She found herself,
As she dropped it all.
Letting it all go,
Letting it all fall.
Fall off.
Fall away.
Everything is gone.
Letting it all go,
Is when she found herself.
Seeing it all.
Seeing it clearly.
Seeing reality,
Without her mask.
Walking away from all that she knew.

Walking away from everything.
This is where,
She found herself.
There she was,
Underneath the pain.
There she was,
Shining a light.
Shining a light...
A light so bright.
She will never allow...
Allow it to dim.
Pulling at her light,
Trying to shut it off...
Trying to dim it...
This will result in her walking away.
She will walk away.
Walk away so fast.
Walk away from it all.
Her light will stay on.
Her light,
Her love.
The love that she found in herself.

Alone

Just me,
All alone.
I listen in silence,
To myself.
I listen to my intuition.
I listen to my inner guidance.
I listen to my inner feedback.
I love to just listen,
In complete stillness.
Here I am,
All alone.
In my awakening,
By myself.
I love everything,
That I've found.
Being alone,
I found myself.
It is when I am alone,
I don't need anything else.
I can be content,
All by myself.
It didn't used to be this way,
That's for sure.
I played the part well,
But I was hiding so much pain.
I can now be alone,
And love every minute.
I can now be alone,
Without my mask.
I can now be alone...

And trust myself,
Fully.
I can now be alone,
And hold my whole heart.
Facing my void,
Showed me my soul.
This new girl,
That has emerged.
She is fierce.
She is brave.
She is strong.
She is full of love.
She is different,
Than she was before.
Some don't see her,
For who she is now.
That's okay,
Because the only person now...
That she needs to be seen by,
Is her.

I Am Not You

It took a long time,
To learn what would make me happy.
It took a long time to know,
That this was in my hands.
It took a long time,
To find my voice.
It was buried down,
Deep inside.
It took a long time to realize,
I am not you.
I can do things that you don't like.
I can try things you would never try.
I can say things to you,
That you don't agree with.
I can say no if I want to say no.
I can go where I want to go.
I can be whoever I want to be.
And none of this,
Has anything to do with you.
This is about me.
If I don't feel like talking,
I don't have to answer.
If I don't feel like seeing you,
I can just stay home.
If I don't feel like listening,
I can decline.
If I can't be there for your feelings,
I can say so.
I can set boundaries.
I can speak the truth.

I can be honest,
Because that is what is best for me.
I can take space,
If that is what I need.
And none of this has anything to do with you.
This is about me.
Some may hear this as selfish.
Or maybe even rude.
But I am learning,
That this is all self-care.
And what is okay with me,
May not be what is okay with you.
Not everyone will like me.
Not everyone will approve.
But that is not my job,
To worry about you.
Finding what my needs are,
Because all I knew was meeting yours.
I would learn that this is my job,
To worry about me.
I am responsible for me,
And you are responsible for you.
If I want to make a change,
I can.
If I want to go in a different direction,
I will.
If I want to change my life,
I can do it.
If I want to say something,
I will.
And if I have a different view,
That is okay.

Because I am me,
I am not you.
It took me my whole life to learn,
That I can be whoever I want to be.
I don't have to ask permission.
I don't have to say why.
I don't have to explain.
I don't have to people please.
I can stand up for myself,
Even when people disapprove.
I don't have to stay.
I can honor myself,
By walking away.
If something doesn't feel right,
I can make a choice.
If something isn't working,
I can let it go.
I don't need to be controlled.
I don't need to be guilted.
I don't need to be manipulated.
And I don't need to be punished,
Just because I am not you.
I finally learned how to be treated,
And unconditionally loved.
That to go back into a world,
Filled with conditions...
I just cannot go that way.
There is a new path,
That has been paved...
Just for me.
It has not been easy,
I had to prove to myself.

That I am worthy when I do nothing at all.
I am worthy,
Just as I am.
That I cannot go back,
To a world of transactions.
If I do this for you,
You do this for me.
That is not how I will live.
I am worthy when I do for me,
Not just when I do for you.
It seems like I was punished,
When I wouldn't meet your needs.
And that needed to end,
On this new journey.
I find the way that I am,
The new me that I found.
I will do for you,
Just because.
I don't need anything in return.
I just want to give.
Because that is me,
That is who I am.
And I love this girl.
I worked so hard to leave,
The only world I ever knew.
And none of this has anything to do with you.
This is me.
This is me now.
In this new world that I have found,
There's kindness and love.
There's respect and freedom.
There are no expectations,

And people just let me be.
No one tries to control me.
I can use my voice,
Whenever I want.
And if I want to retreat to my own little world,
That is not looked down on.
And none of this,
Has anything to do with you.
This was me,
Finding myself.
Underneath all the layers.
Leaving a world that wouldn't allow,
Me to have my own identity.
This path that I found,
It was a journey of grief.
This path that I found,
It was a journey of loving who I am.
Every single part,
And who I used to be,
And then letting her go.
Now I can finally see.
It was time for a new girl to show.
I know it hurt the people who loved her,
Because they were not ready for her to leave.
I am so sorry for taking her away from you.
And I am thankful for all the love that you gave.
It is time for her to go now.
And be someone new.
And none of this has anything to do with you.
This is about me,
And the vision that I saw.
Everything I wanted,

Was right in front of me.
It felt so far away.
I knew I had to get there,
But I didn't know how.
Until I found this path of self-love.
While on this path that I chose,
I would sometimes look back.
I would miss my old world,
But I knew that wasn't my path.
I had to keep going,
No matter what.
I had to continue,
As hard as it was.
I would cry a lot,
And I learned that is okay.
This new world accepted my tears.
This new world accepted my fears.
This new world accepted my flaws.
I finally took my rose-colored glasses off.
And then I could see,
Everything that was for me.
Those glasses were a false reality.
As I saw everything for what it was,
I had to accept,
All that had happened.
I had to see what was real,
And then I had to feel.
I kept it all in,
I didn't even know.
My heart was hidden,
With so many walls.
On this new path,

I opened my heart.
And then everything around me
Started to change.
This was my new life,
My new start.
This was about me.
This was never about you.
Because this was the girl,
That I was always meant to be.
And I learned to love her, completely.
It took a lot of hardship,
And a lot of pain and tears.
But I know at the end of this path,
Will be joy and love.
That is what will be there waiting.
I just had to move through all of the other emotions.
The emotions, in the way.
The journey of my self-love,
And my authentic self.
It Is a path of undoing and letting go.
I can undo anything I choose.
I can learn new ways.
I can start fresh,
I just had to go deep inside.
There was so much there,
That I never even knew.
And none of this had anything to do with you.
This was me,
Becoming real.
Real with myself.
Real with everyone else.
No more hiding.

No more sacrificing myself for others.
No more pretending.
No more pleasing.
The people on this journey with me,
These are the people who finally see me.
I finally feel seen.
I finally feel heard.
These are the people that understand,
That this was never about any of them.
They are on their own journey,
Whichever way they go.
Their path may look different than mine.
But this is the beauty of life.
That we all have our own path,
That we all must follow.
Follow, to be whoever we want to be.
I will give my support,
And I will send all of my love...
To all of you,
Who are finding your own path.
It is not easy,
And it is unknown.
None of us know what we are doing.
None of us know what each day will bring.
I will learn surrender,
On my path.
I will stop putting my faith,
In other people's hands.
Because I will learn that the way people behave,
It has to do with them...
And it is not about me.
I will find faith.

I will find God.
I will find nature.
I will find my higher power.
And I will trust and embrace the unknown,
And surrender to all that is meant for me.
I will fix my relationship with change.
Because in order to go where I want to go,
I will have to change everything I know.
Everything I knew,
And everything I was.
It will all have to change.
It will all have to be removed.
We all are who we are,
Because of our pasts.
We are made up of puzzle pieces,
Of each experience.
And at any given moment,
We can start to remove each puzzle piece,
And replace it with something new.
It is up to us,
To choose a new future.
To move forward,
We can't be in the past.
We need to learn skills,
To accept and let go.
And in this new future,
It is up to me.
What is next?
I am not sure.
All I know,
Is that I am learning,
To love this new me.

She is brave and she is free.
This was always about me,
And all that was meant to be.
This was never about you.
This was about me.
I hope that one day, you will understand.
I hope that one day, you will see.
I hope that one day,
You will send love.
To this new me,
Who still holds so much love for you.

Integration

Have you ever met,
Every part of yourself?
Have you ever actually sat,
And listened to all of your parts?
Parts of yourself.
There are so many parts.
Each one,
Has something to say.
If you sit quietly,
In complete silence.
If you start to listen,
And give up control.
If you sit in solitude,
And breathe.
You will start to hear all of your parts.
They all have a story.
They all have something to say.
They live inside,
Of your heart.
The part of me when I was 4.
There is a part of me when I was 10.
This part of me when I was 6.
This part of me when I was 8.
They all have never met.
These parts of myself,
I have dismissed.
I didn't acknowledge,
Or listen.
It is in silence,
That I start to hear,

All of my parts.
They are all here.
They are all waiting.
Waiting to be healed.
And integrated,
Into my full self.
This is what I know as wholeness.
This is my work,
To become whole.
Stop looking for someone,
To complete me.
The only way,
To complete myself.
Is to heal,
All of these parts.
Once I started to listen,
All of my feelings started to come up.
The feelings that I suppressed.
The feelings that I ignored.
The feelings that I dismissed,
Or didn't want to hear.
As I started to listen,
To all of these parts...
They slowly started to feel heard and seen.
They slowly started to trust me.
As the trust was built,
And they felt safe...
They all started to integrate.
This became a process,
That I started to embrace.
There was a part,
From when I was 14,

That carried so much pain.
All of it needed,
To be seen and felt.
It all needed,
To be understood.
Given compassion,
And nurture.
This was one of the biggest parts,
Of myself that needed so much attention.
As I gave this part,
More and more love...
I took away her pain.
And helped her feel seen.
A part of me,
That lived inside,
Was always told that she was bad.
Everything she did,
Was because she just wanted to be...
Loved and nurtured.
This part of me felt rejected.
For so many years.
She never felt seen.
She never felt heard.
She was never asked.
She was never hugged.
She never felt loved.
She was only pushed away,
To the side.
She was punished and rejected,
And even ignored.
She lived inside of me,
All of these years.

Crying out for help,
Living in fear.
This little part needed to be held.
She needed support.
She needed guidance.
This little part was never shown.
She was never given what she needed.
It took years,
To hear her.
It started,
As a small whisper.
Slowly, she got louder and louder.
Until I no longer could ignore her.
I finally heard her.
This whisper,
I heard.
Now I sit,
With her and listen.
I say,
I hear you.
I see you.
I ask how you are.
I understand now,
That this is all that you needed.
I understand now,
It was as simple as that.
This is when I look,
At little children around me.
And I notice that,
This is all that they need.
They all need love.
They all need to be seen and heard.

They all need to feel understood.
We all have little children inside of us.
We can call them children.
Or we can call them parts.
They all need to feel heard and seen.
Never ignored.
This can take years,
It is not an overnight thing.
It is a process.
This is the work.
As I sit,
And I listen.
I also have to feel.
Feel these feelings I never felt.
Feel these feelings I have ignored.
Ignored for so long.
For so many years.
Feel them as they come up.
I pushed these feelings away,
Because I didn't know.
I didn't know how to feel.
I just wasn't shown.
I will feel it all,
Because she is worth it.
She was just a little girl,
Who felt all alone.
This little girl,
Has made me strong.
She is amazing.
She has been all along.
She never believed it,
Until now.

Because I am giving her all that she needs.
She now feels worthy.
All these years,
She never felt good enough.
She didn't feel seen.
She didn't feel heard.
She never felt loved.
Loved unconditionally.
She made herself small,
Because that is what she was taught.
Make yourself small.
Be controlled.
Never use your voice.
Never stand up for yourself.
You will be punished,
If you speak up.
If you use your voice,
You will be scolded.
You will be left,
If you make a mistake.
This is what she was told.
This is what she was shown.
Because the adults in her life,
Proved all of this to be right.
They told her these things.
They showed her these things.
They blamed her.
They made her believe,
That she was always wrong.
And if she messed up,
She would never be asked why.
She would never try to be understood.

She would just be labeled,
And called bad.
She would be blamed,
And then she'd be left.
She lived her whole life,
Believing this to be true.
She lived her whole life,
Letting others label her.
Never being taught.
Never being forgiven.
It was her fault.
She was to blame.
She lived her whole life,
Letting others give her an identity.
An identity that was never hers,
To begin with.
She lived her whole life,
Being projected on.
By others who couldn't see themselves.
They couldn't see them.
They would only see her.
In a way that was distorted.
In a way that wasn't aligned,
With who she really was.
This was all keeping her,
From finding her light.
Until one day,
She said enough is enough.
She started to make changes.
She started to notice.
That this was not,
How she should have been treated.

One day she decided,
That this is not okay.
This will not go on,
Things will have to change.
She changed her voice.
She changed her words.
She changed her tone.
She started to walk away,
From anything one sided.
She started to walk away,
From blatant disrespect.
She will not stay.
Not anymore.
For people who walk,
All over her.
She has learned boundaries.
And her own needs.
And she started to appreciate.
She would appreciate,
That she never fit in.
She would appreciate,
That she was the black sheep.
She would appreciate,
That she could stand on her own.
She would appreciate all of her wounds.
Because it is in her wounds,
That she found herself.
She found gratitude and strength.
She found wisdom and courage.
She found all of this,
And started to heal.
And as all of these parts began to heal,

She started to feel...
More empowered.
It was in this empowerment,
That she began to see a whole new life.
This integration helped her to see,
That there was more for her.
She started to believe,
More and more.
That this old world was no longer for her.
She will move on,
As she slips into this new identity.
This is when she sees,
Everything so clear.
In this integration.
In this awakening.
This is when she says,
"This is everything I am.
And all that I want.
This new identity.
This is what was meant to be.
The rest of my life,
Is right in front of me."

This Space.

In between spaces...
Is something that isn't talked about,
A lot.
Who am I here?
What is this space?
Does it have a name?
Go from place to place,
But what is in between?
What do I do here?
How do I live?
Do I make a decision?
Do I jump?
Or do I stay?
Do I leap?
Or do I stay?
This space of in between...
Of who I was,
And who I am going to be.
This is the space that I am in.
In which, I can't describe this feeling.
It is the space,
Of who I was,
And who I'm going to be.
This is the space,
That holds all of the fear.
All of the fear,
That I have never seen.
I have never been here before.
I don't know how to navigate.
This is out of my comfort zone.

This is where I am supposed to grow.
Everything is new.
It doesn't feel the same.
I feel so insecure.
This is how I know,
That this space is right.
I am not where I want to be.
But I can feel that it is not far off,
Until I am ready.
That is how I know,
That this space is for me.
I can feel it in my body.
I am supposed to be here.
I will trust this.
This place that I am in,
Is just a space.
Is this where I decide?
Is this my destiny?
Is this my calling?
Is this where I find my purpose?
Is this where I find meaning?
I keep waiting,
For a feeling.
I keep pausing,
This is so confusing.
I can feel,
That it is not far off...
It is getting really close.
But close to what?
The next space?
What is this space?
Is it a place?

Where am I supposed to go?
This is the place,
Where surrender is.
And that is what I will do.
Surrender everything,
And all of it.
And trust that I will feel,
Exactly what is meant for me.
What I've been waiting for.
It is true...
That good things come with time.
And good things come to those who wait.
So, this must be the space that I am in.
It feels like a waiting room.
Waiting for my new life to start.
I just don't know when that will be.
It is in surrender,
That all of that will come.
And it will feel right.
Until that time,
I will wait.
Patiently.
In this space.
This is where the work is done.
All the letting go.
This is where the wishes come,
And all of my ideas.
Believing and manifesting.
They say,
All of your dreams will come to life,
If you just let everything go.
I used to not know,

What that meant.
But it finally makes sense.
All you have to do,
Is give up everything.
Let it all go.
Walk into the unknown.
Keep the faith.
Keep the trust.
And feel the deep inner knowing.
Connect with my body.
Be still and know,
In this space.
This is where I am.
The place that I am in,
Is just a space.
A transition.

It Is Her Or Me

There is the girl that I am,
And the girl that I was.
People see her.
People look at her.
She talks.
She works.
She listens.
These people see just one girl.
These people see this same girl,
That they've always seen.
They look at her,
The way they always have.
And they think it is,
The girl that they've always known.
This is the girl,
That they all love.
But I am not her,
Not anymore.
I have to make a choice.
To leave her behind.
To become who I am,
I must choose myself.
When I make this choice,
It might mean letting people down.
Because it is her that they see.
It is her that they love.
I love her too,
But her time has come.
That she must go and allow me to lead.
I can't choose both.

I can't be both.
And right now,
It feels like that's what I am.
Right now, it feels like I am living two different lives.
One that is hers,
And one that is mine.
There are people that see the growth.
They cheer me on.
And then there are the people,
That want me to go back and be that other girl.
It is a fight that I must win.
But in order to win,
I must give her up.
There is a rope.
A rope,
That I am holding on to.
The more time that goes by,
My grip is loosening up.
I can't keep holding on.
It's holding me back.
Who am I doing this for?
I must let go...
Of this rope that is connecting me with her.
I must choose me,
Over her.
The time is near,
The time has come.
I must make the choice.
This choice is mine,
It is her or me.
What will it be?
It is her, that got me this far.

It is her, that has carried me through.
It is her, that I have relied on.
So how can I let her go?
It is her that's been there,
Through everything.
It is her that made me strong.
It is her that lifted me up.
It is her that I love.
So how can I leave her?
She is proud,
And she led me here...
Just for me to shine.
She's known all along.
She knows that there is more for me.
And she has brought me here.
She knew my grip,
Would be loose someday.
She just didn't know,
It would be now.
She didn't know,
It would feel like this.
She didn't know.
It would feel like death.
She had no idea,
How it would feel.
All she knew is,
All things come to an end.
The end is here,
And she must go.
There is so much,
That lies ahead.
There is so much,

Waiting for me.
This is my future.
This is my freedom.
This is my destiny.
The time is now here.
That I must make the choice.
Let go of the rope.
Let go of her.
It is her or me.
What will I choose?
It is a new era.
It is a new time.
And she must stay,
Back in this old world.
I must leave her,
In my past.
I must go.
I say goodbye.
I leave her now,
I send to her,
So much love.
And I will let go of my grip.
I let go of everything,
That is connected to her.
It is now her that is left.
I move forward,
Without her.
As I take some steps,
I take along my fear.
And I look back.
To see,
This beautiful girl,

Standing there looking out at me.

"Be brave."

Look Forward.
Uncover
Your wounds.
Walk through the fire.
Embrace your Soul,
Everything...
You desire.
.Serenity.
.Will be.
.Waiting.

Who's That?

Who's that?
I don't know her.
I don't know her, not anymore.
I left her behind.
She feels so distant.
She feels like a different girl.
That's because she is.
She is different.
She is not the same.
She feels so vague.
She's pretty far away.
Far away from me.
Far away,
In the distance.
Far away,
I can't reach.
I can't even reach her,
To try to be her again.
I can't even pretend,
I can't do that again.
I had to decide,
To leave her behind.
I had to let go.
Let go of her hand.
I had to release her.
Release her,
And go.
I went ahead,
And she stayed back.
The problem is,

There are so many that loved her.
The problem is,
People don't understand.
The problem is,
I won't go back.
I won't go back,
To be her again.
I will step forward.
I will keep moving.
I will keep becoming.
Becoming new.
Becoming me.
Becoming this girl,
That most people don't know.
I know her.
I know her well.
I've gotten to know her.
I've put my time in.
Alone.
Solitude.
Quiet and peace.
This is where I grew.
Grew into me.
This where I left, that old girl.
Left her behind,
And found my soul.
This is where I loved, all of my parts.
This is where I became whole.
This is where I left that girl.
Left her behind,
And found someone new.
This someone new.

This new me.
This new girl.
Who's that?
This is me.
This is me, now.
That old girl is gone.

Half of Myself

Half of me.
Walking around.
Half of me.
The other half,
A void.
A space.
An emptiness.
A void of pain.
A void of misery.
A void of agony.
A complete lack of love.
Half of me.
Walking around.
Half of me.
Trying to find love.
Half of me.
Trying to figure myself out.
Half of me.
Trying to make a life.
All with this void.
That took up half of myself.
This void needed attention.
It needed care.
It needed the other half of me,
To give nurturing and love.
This void,
Needed time.
This void,
Needed me.
This half of myself,

Needed to be filled up.
This half of me,
Needed distractions to leave.
This half of me,
Needed to find worth.
This half of me,
Needed to be filled with my own self-love.
These two halves,
They worked together.
These two halves,
Learned from each other.
That other half,
Had to listen.
Had to listen,
To that darkness.
That other half,
Had to release.
Release the pain and agony.
This whole ordeal,
Took a lot of time.
It was not an overnight thing.
That other half of me,
Needed to believe.
Needed to believe,
In this process.
That other half of me,
Needed to trust.
Needed to trust and surrender.
That other half of me,
Needed to give up and lose.
Lose, everything it knew.
That other half,

Had so much fear.
Fear of the unknown.
Fear of change.
That other half,
Was so empty.
That other half,
Was filling up,
Externally.
Fill up with people.
Fill up with plans.
Fill up with noise.
Fill up with happiness.
It needed quiet.
It needed space.
It needed alone time.
It needed solitude.
This other half was trying to avoid.
Just find happiness,
And it'll just replace.
No.
No.
Face the pain.
Face the misery.
Feel it and heal it.
Then,
Comes love.
Then,
Comes happiness.
Happiness is just a sensation.
It is not a destination.
I really understand,
What that means now.

Happiness is fleeting,
It comes and it goes.
But love,
Is always.
Love is in me.
It is a process.
It is within.
This half of myself,
Is now a whole.
This whole.
My whole self.
She no longer,
Will accept what is not for her.
She has these standards.
She has this love.
She has this wholeness,
That can't be split,
Not ever again.
She cried so many tears.
She's left so much behind.
This wholeness,
Is hers.
This wholeness,
Is here.
Here to stay.

Fire

The chaos.
The flames.
The heat.
Everything is on fire.
Scorching.
Roaring.
Smoky.
It's spreading,
Through parts of me...
Parts of my life.
Keep going,
Be brave.
Walk
Through
It
All.
It needs to come.
Come to an end.
It's okay...
It's okay to fall.
Get back up again.
More fire.
This heat.
This smog.
Can't breathe.
Spreading.
Everything I knew,
Is gone.
Flames.
All I could see.

Burning.
Blazing.
Right in front of me.
Clear it all away.
Until there is an empty space.
Everything is gone.
Cleansing.
Pure.
Clear.
What will I put here?
After the flames,
And my walk through it all,
This big open space.
I can finally breathe.
Do I replace what was here?
With what?
Clean Air.
So Soft.
I love it here.

I Am Sorry

I am so sorry.
I am sorry for not hearing you,
When you had something to say.
I am sorry for not seeing you,
When you needed to be seen.
All this time,
Trying to be seen by everyone else.
All this time,
Trying to be heard by everyone else.
You sent me the signals,
But I didn't know what you meant.
We haven't been aligned,
For such a long time.
But now,
I hear you.
I see you.
I know your language.
It was me all along,
That you were longing for.
Longing for someone else to come and save me.
Longing for someone to hold my heart.
Longing for someone who was here all along.
That someone was me.
We were in the wrong world,
For so many years.
I was surrounded by people,
Leaning on me.
I was too busy…
Worrying about them,
Without having boundaries.

This was what was familiar,
And shown to me.
While I was giving love,
To everyone else...
You were being neglected.
You needed care.
You were crying out,
It got so loud.
It got to where you were screaming.
I am so sorry you had to yell.
I didn't even know how to take care of you.
All I was taught,
Was to be there for everyone else.
We just had to learn,
Together,
We figured it out.
Thank you for pointing all of this out.
We are slowly finding,
Where we need to be.
We will find which way to go.
I hear you now,
Loud and clear.
I vow to you,
I will always be here.

This Bridge

I look at this bridge,
Ahead of me.
I put one foot in front of me,
And take a step.
Just one step.
It is wobbly.
It is windy.
It is turbulent.
This storm on this bridge...
Don't worry,
It's not permanent.
Keep going.
Take another step.
Walk through the storm,
Just keep taking another breath.
Breathe in,
Breathe out.
It's okay.
Take another step,
This storm won't stay.
This bridge will take me,
To another place.
This storm will prepare me,
For what is next.
This bridge is a path,
It can feel scary.
This bridge doesn't feel safe,
It's not very sturdy.
This storm will pass,
And I will feel brave.

Now, it is fire,
That I see.
I am walking into fire,
With only myself.
How do I survive?
How do I not have a meltdown?
Close your eyes,
And just keep going.
It is how you walk,
Through those flames.
Have patience,
And trust yourself.
It feels so uncomfortable.
This heat. This smoke.
On this bridge.
This fire,
It'll pass too,
Just wait and see...
Take the risk.
Take a breath,
And always keep going.
The fire is almost behind you,
Your walk will be worth it.
I made it, I did it,
I made it through!
This gave me strength,
To keep walking on this bridge.
What's next for me,
On this journey?
Another storm is ahead.
It won't feel as bad,
I bet.

This next storm is really bad.
But I've found faith,
And I hold on to that.
I keep breathing,
Through it all.
Next thing I know,
The storm is gone.
Another storm.
Another fire.
Another storm.
Another fire.
Crossing this bridge,
Is really hard.
It's not really what I desired.
Darkness has passed,
And I finally see light.
I can see the end of this bridge.
This new place has color,
It is so welcoming.
This new place has light,
And love shines through.
I feel it,
My heart is opening.
My heart opens to this light.
I feel the love,
Everything feels right.
I step off the bridge,
And I look back.
My god,
What an impact.
Tears fall from my eyes.

I hold my heart,
And send that old world love and light...
From this new place.

Goodbye

Saying goodbye used to be,
The hardest thing I ever had to do.
The more I let go,
The easier it became.
And the more me,
I would see.
Saying goodbye...
Meant walking away.
This is the end,
I can no longer stay.
I will make a life,
That I deserve.
I will make a life that I was always meant to live.
And if saying goodbye is what is meant to be,
I will turn my back,
And I will leave.
Goodbye is hard.
But staying where you no longer fit,
Will tear you apart.
I will go where I belong,
As long as it takes me to find.
It really did take me a long time.
I followed my inner knowing.
My intuition.
And trusted in where I was going.
I looked to the sky, the stars,
And the moon.
With each step,
I kept moving forward.
It was in those goodbyes,

That showed me the light.
I followed the light,
I followed my heart.
And trusted the signs,
That were shown.
The signs were always there,
For me to see.
I just had to look,
I just had to believe.
Believe in yourself,
The vision will come.
The road to go down won't be easy.
The road to travel on won't be carved out.
But if you follow your intuition,
Your life will come about.
Saying goodbye will be a continuous struggle,
To reach where you have to go.
Change will be constant.
Keep looking ahead.
Without looking back.
Saying goodbye is a reminder,
That you are heading towards the light.
Not everyone will come,
Not everyone will understand.
It is up to you,
To find acceptance in that.
Goodbye is a word,
That used to be so hard.
It used to not be used,
In my vocabulary.
I will hold on so tight,
Until my whole self was sacrificed.

Until I wasn't growing at all.
All because I couldn't say,
The words goodbye.
And leave behind,
People who were in my life.
People who meant the world to me,
But we were just on different paths.
No matter what I did,
I could no longer feel the connection.
It was breaking me,
By holding on to them.
So, I finally had to let go.
They all felt so far,
Away from me.
It felt like I was being completely weighed down.
It was not their fault.
It was just that,
I had to keep moving forward.
To follow what was right for me.
I had a vision,
That was like a magnet.
It kept drawing me,
Closer and closer.
It was so hard.
To feel these emotions.
That come with leaving everything behind.
I didn't know,
What was waiting for me.
But I will keep going,
It is time to leave.
Goodbye to you,
And even me.

Saying goodbye
To it all...
Meant saying goodbye,
To parts of me.
Goodbye meant,
Disconnection.
Goodbye meant,
Reconnection.
Goodbye is really bittersweet.
Goodbye is followed by new hello's.
Goodbye means,
A new beginning.
Goodbye means,
Another era.
Another chapter.
It is time.
I've said my goodbyes,
As a new page turns.
I will turn the page,
With no regrets...
And understand,
Goodbye is a mindset.

Raw

That saying,
The truth hurts.
No one likes the truth.
Raw words.
Real.
I love the truth.
We live in a fake world.
I used to live there.
A world filled with impressing and glamour.
Smiles and laughter.
What do you have?
What do you own?
What do you do?
How come no one ever asks,
Who are you?
Who are you inside?
Underneath the money.
Underneath the façade?
Who are you,
Underneath it all?
How come no one ever asks,
What does your heart look like?
Why don't people say,
Tell me about your spirit.
Tell me about your soul.
Instead, it is all,
What do you do for work?
How much did that cost?
What do you own?
What do you have to show?

I don't want to know,
Any of that.
It is not important.
Not to me.
It is surface.
What is beyond,
The surface?
I want to be real.
I want to go deep.
I want more.
I want raw.
I want to know things like,
Who is your mentor?
Who do you look up to?
Why are you the way you are?
Tell me all of your pain.
Tell me what you've learned.
Give me information.
Give me what's inside.
Anything external is not who you really are.
Who are you really?
Anything on the outside,
It doesn't even count.
Tell me what's within.
Tell me your dreams.
Tell me your goals.
I want to know your values.
Let's have a real conversation.
Let's talk truth.
Let's talk struggle.
Let's talk about how you are feeling.
Let's get naked.

Naked with words.
Let's be raw.
Difficult topics can lead to connection.
We can talk religion,
And if it is different than mine,
That's okay.
I don't have to agree with your politics.
We don't have to get worked up,
We can just accept.
I accept that,
That is your truth.
I will tell you mine,
We don't have to be the same.
Why do people not enjoy,
Hearing other sides?
Why does everything have to be a fight?
We don't have to agree.
Let me speak my truth.
Let me speak.
I'll let you...
Do the same.
Raw and real.
Let me be honest.
Hear me out.
It is true,
The truth can hurt.
But it is more true,
Hiding hurts more.
The truth can reveal what is being hidden.
What is being pushed down inside of you.
Is this why people struggle with the truth?
People don't want to look,

At what that they are pushing down?
Or they don't want to use their mind,
To dig deep?
That used to be me.
Eventually everything comes out.
Our world needs more truth tellers.
Our world needs more love.
Our word needs less,
Judgement.
Tell me what you think,
Don't hold back.
The truth can make us better,
The truth can reveal.
It can reveal what we can't see in ourselves.
So, find those people.
Find the raw people.
Keep them.
Challenge them.
Let them speak.
Hear them.
Accept them.
And always,
Hold space,
For the truth.
It is raw.
It is real.
That is what I want.
That is what I will live for.

Rose-Colored Glasses

I wore these rose-colored glasses for years.
Those glasses made life look easy.
These glasses made life look fun.
These glasses made,
Everyone happy.
These glasses made,
Everything appear positive.
The world is full of joy.
And only joy.
Good.
Everything is good...
All the time.
These glasses,
I would learn...
Brought an altered reality.
What happens when,
You take them off?
Let me tell you...
The
Glasses
Come
Off.
That vision with them on,
Was a world full of denial.
Everything is just,
As it is now.
Without them on.
This is reality.
Everything is real.
There Is still good,

But everything is different.
Everything feels different.
Without the glasses,
There are flaws.
There is negativity.
There are problems,
That will need to be solved.
There are difficult conversations.
There is inward work,
That needs to be done.
There is reflecting,
And tears.
There is sorrow,
And joy.
There is indecisiveness.
There is self-awareness.
There is anger and regret.
There is love and laughter.
There is confusion.
Mixed
With denial and projection.
There is no more perfection.
It is a rollercoaster.
Those glasses kept everything perfect.
The lenses turned,
Everything to perfection.
Without those glasses,
I see clear now.
Without those glasses,
I come out of the illusion.
Life was an illusion,
With these glasses.

This was a shocking discovery,
For me.
Can I live,
Without these glasses?
Can I keep going,
Without this rose-colored lens?
These glasses made,
Everything distorted.
How could I not have known,
The whole time I was wearing them?
These rose-colored glasses,
Brought safety to me.
They helped me feel safe.
So, without them,
I must create that in a different way.
My world was all,
An illusion.
Without the illusion,
What do I see?
I see reality.
And this new reality,
Can't be seen through these rose-colored glasses.
I am on the other side now.
Looking out at others,
Still wearing these rose-colored lenses.
I see them,
But they can't see me.
Because they are living in that altered reality.
I feel like I am looking at a rose-colored world.
It is so clear,
That all of these people,
Have rose colored eyes.

It is a separation now.
A separation of people who wear these glasses.
And the people who have chosen to take them off.
I have discovered that taking them off,
It is a much bumpier road.
Taking them off brings difficult conversations.
Taking them off,
Brings growth.
Taking them off,
Allows you to go deeper.
With not just yourself,
But with others as well.
Taking them off,
Brought connection.
Taking them off,
Brought clarity.
Taking them off,
Brought reality.
Taking them off,
Brought freedom.

It is inside.

The darkness.
Is inside.
But the light
Is too.
The why's.
The how's.
The who's.
The where's.
It is all inside.
Where to?
It is within.
Do I stop?
It is inside.
Do I stay?
It is within you.
Ask yourself questions.
Be brave.
It will be uncomfortable.
The light is underneath,
All of the darkness.
Understanding
And
Compassion.
It is within.
Anytime you feel lonely,
It is a time,
To sit with yourself.
The loneliness is,
Calling you.
It is confusing,

When the loneliness comes.
We think we need people,
Our family,
Technology.
We keep looking,
Externally.
Surround ourselves,
With happiness.
We think we need,
Something to make us better.
Surround and uplift ourselves.
Fix it.
No one tells us...
To sit in it.
But we think it is,
On the outside.
Everything we need,
Is on the inside.
Our hearts.
We forget about our hearts.
Our unconscious.
There is so much,
In our unconscious.
Our inner dialogue.
Tune in.
It can be changed.
Our body is so powerful.
But so many run away,
From our own body.
Our body is so powerful.
We choose survival mode,
Over being connected to our body.

Our body stores darkness.
It stores the light.
It stores love.
Our body is made to move.
Move this energy.
Move it out.
It is made to heal.
It is made to breathe.
Movement and bending.
It is in the movement,
You will tune in.
It is in the breath,
You will tune in.
Do you hear it?
That inner feedback.
Be in it.
Be in your body.
Let everything flow,
Let everything be.
Let everything come,
Let everything leave.
Just stay in it.
Let the energy flow.
Let it come,
Let the feelings go.
Feel the wind,
Soak up the sun.
Feel the breeze,
Go all in.
The sky and the stars.
Feel the earth on your feet.
Feel the dirt in between your toes.

Go to the ocean,
Let the waves wash up on your legs.
The water will calm you.
The water is healing.
The sky above,
And the stars,
They're always there
To reach for.
The earth is constant.
Your body is all you have.
Your heart and soul live within.
It is love that will carry you.
It is love that will ground you.
That love is inside.
That love is within.
Stay grounded.
Connect with your body.
Love your body.
Everything you need,
Is there.
Inside.

Movement

Your body is made to move.
Your body is energetic.
The energy flows,
When your body moves.
Movement.
Movement brings connection.
Connection to your body.
Connection to your heart.
Connection to your mind.
Connection to your soul.
Movement brings connection.
Connection to yourself.
To move,
Is to connect.
You are connected.
Connected to your body,
Is how you bring healing.
As you move,
There are sensations.
The sensations are energy.
Every feeling,
Every emotion...
Will flow through you with movement.
Movement is healing.
Movement is refreshing.
Movement is cleansing.
Your body is made to move.
So, move it.
Move it slow,
Or move it fast.

Dancing or yoga.
Weightlifting or running.
Walking or swimming.
Any hobby that brings us joy,
Usually has some kind of movement involved.
Movement brings endorphins.
Movement brings health.
Movement brings serenity.
Movement brings release.
Movement brings healing.
Love your body,
Love your movement.
Get out and get moving.

Unconditionally

Little girls should be loved.
Little girls should be taught.
Little girls should be held.
They should be cherished and protected.
They should be stood up for.
They should be honored,
Kissed and hugged more.
Little girls will not be perfect,
They will make mistakes.
They will be devious,
Maybe with an attitude,
And sometimes rebellious.
It is a parent's job to show them the way.
A parent chose to bring them into this world.
A parent made a commitment to have this child,
No matter what.
No matter if she is good,
Or bad.
It is them.
That would help,
To mold who she is.
Show her and guide her,
And lead the way.
Not expect that she's just,
Going to know everything.
Some little girls are good,
Some will need more love.
Punishments. Sometimes.
But abandonment. Never.
Neglect. Never.

Ignored. Never.
Shamed. Never.
Name called. Never.
Manipulated. Never.
Little girls should be handled with care.
Little girls should be chosen by their parents.
Over anyone or any situation.
A little girl should be their number one.
Protect her from harm.
Protect her from hurt.
Protect her, is a parent's job.
She did not ask,
To be born.
It is on the parent.
They are the reason that,
She is here.
A little girl starts as an infant,
Not knowing a single thing.
She grows up,
Looking to her parents for everything.
To show her what's right,
And teach her when she's wrong.
She looks to her parent,
For love and connection.
She looks to her parent,
For guidance.
If a little girl acts out,
Is it love that she's looking for?
If a little girl makes a mistake,
Is it their attention she needs?
It is not a parent's job to react to her actions.
Their reaction is theirs,

Not hers to carry.
When a little girl acts out,
Shouldn't a parent look deeper?
But how do they go deeper,
If they can't look at themselves?
A parent's job is not to project their inner turmoil,
On their little girl.
A parent's job is to take care of themselves,
So that they can take care of her.
They will love themselves,
So that she knows how,
To give herself love.
But when a parent doesn't show her that.
How does she know that it's even possible,
To love herself?
When a parent only loves on condition,
What is that teaching her?
A little girl will go somewhere else,
To find love if she can't find it at home.
If a little girl is not shown how to communicate,
Or given a safe place.
A little girl may try to create it on her own.
This may be in different ways.
If a parent leaves a little girl,
That little girl will never be the same.
A parent's job is to stay.
A parent's job is to find new ways.
A parent's job is,
Not to give her away.
It is a parent's job,
To love unconditionally.
Isn't it a parent's job,

To help that little girl feel loved,
So that she won't hurt anymore?
It is a parent's job,
To try to understand and give compassion.
It is a parent's job to find that hurt,
Inside of that little girl.
But what if that hurt,
Is caused by them?
And they don't want to see,
That they could be wrong.
It is only her,
That is wrong.
She will be blamed.
She will be removed,
From the family.
She will be punished,
Because that is what she deserves.
Mistakes are not okay,
Rebellion is forbidden.
This will all be thrown in her face.
Every little girl will have her struggles.
Every little girl should have support.
The support from a parent is something,
That she cannot find anywhere else.
The love from a parent is something,
That she cannot find anywhere else.
Love and support,
Should come from a parent.
But if they're not giving that to themselves,
How do they give it to her?
A little girl needs her mother to choose her,
Nurture and stand up for her.

Love her, unconditionally.
A little girl needs her father to choose her,
Protect her.
Love her, unconditionally.
Little girls will not be perfect.
Little girls will have flaws.
Little girls will mess up.
Little girls should not be left.
Little girls should not be ignored.
Little girls should be kept.
Little girls should be loved.
That little girl will choose herself.
That little girl will protect herself.
That little girl has a heart,
She has followed it from the very start.
That little girl will love.
And be loved unconditionally.
She will make that happen,
She will take the lead.

Black and White

She left a world of black and white,
And she found a beautiful world full of greys.
Her old world was full,
Of nevers and always.
Her old world was,
This way or that way.
Her old world was,
You do this or you do that,
Or you don't get anything.
If you don't act this way,
This will happen.
There was never an in between.
Her old world was,
Very extreme.
She didn't know any other way.
But she woke up one day,
And decided that she needed to see more of the grey.
The world of black and white kept her feeling safe.
This was all that she knew.
Her personality was also,
Black and white.
Very extreme.
She'd dip her foot out into the world...
And if there was something that didn't work for her,
She went the other way.
She would learn that in this new world,
She could be whatever she wanted to be.
In the world of black and white,
She could only be one way.
If she became something different,

She would be questioned or even scolded.
Why can't I just be what I want to be?
Why can't I say what I want to say?
She didn't even know that she was in this,
Black and white world.
This was why nothing would work for her.
Her views would have to change,
And her mind and heart would have to open.
She started to see so many more colors.
So many more hues,
So many more greys.
As she found this new world,
The people who lived in that black and white world,
Just did not understand.
They thought it was about them,
Instead of asking her to explain.
If they had asked her questions,
She would have explained.
That she found this new world,
Full of opportunity.
This new world,
And these new shades,
Brought to her many new ways.
The people in her old world wouldn't ask her questions,
It felt more like expectations and assumptions,
And she wasn't accepted.
She would find in this new world full of grey,
She could go with the flow.
She could leave,
Or stay.
She could just be.
She would start to accept people the way they are.

She'd observe more,
And react less.
She'd leave her control in that black and white world.
She'd replace her control with understanding and
Compassion.
This new world also showed her forgiveness.
The world of black and white,
Everything was either good or bad.
Everything had a reaction.
And this new world of grey,
It would be letting everything come,
Then letting it all go.
Trusting and surrender,
Using words to communicate.
And if people don't like it,
They can leave.
If people leave,
It's okay.
In the world of black and white,
You just had to stay.
In this new world full of grey,
People come and people go.
It is a part of life.
That lesson she had to learn,
A thousand times.
This world of black and white would invite her back
sometimes,
And she would decline.
She loved this new world.
In this new world,
Is where she found love for herself.

The Mask

Act like you are happy,
Even when you're not.
Put a smile on your face,
No matter what.
We don't talk about the bad things.
We don't say the truth.
We put on our masks.
For everyone to see.
But behind that mask,
Is the real me.
That mask was conditioned,
From when I was little.
That mask was made to please my parents.
And to protect me from any kind of pain.
That mask will be worn,
While out in public,
And even at home.
Now everyone knows and loves,
This mask that I've worn.
Everyone thinks that is really me,
And when I start to take it off,
I feel relieved.
I might be the only one,
Because everyone around me,
Seems to want that mask back on.
That mask that I wore for so many years,
Was mainly put on out of fear.
I walked on eggshells,
A lot as a little girl.
I had to act a certain way,

To receive love.
I had to act a certain way,
So that they would be pleased.
I had to act a certain way,
To not trigger my parents.
And if I did,
It was always my fault.
Silent treatment and ignoring was the way.
Passive aggressive was what was shown.
Walking on eggshells every day.
Don't upset them, okay?
You must act nice,
And always happy.
Please them to receive,
Any kind of love.
Guilt trips and sarcasm,
Was the norm.
Shaming and blaming would make them laugh.
That's the way,
That got them through.
Those are the only ways that they knew.
Never discuss or talk anything out.
Shove it away,
And act the same.
You must always act the same,
And never change.
You must put on the show,
And do for them.
Always what was best for them.
Become the nice girl,
Become small.
Become who they love,

Don't mess up.
Be the emotional support,
And be the lifter.
Nothing was ever about me,
I couldn't safely express anything.
Sure, I had the cool clothes and a big house.
Money and vacations,
I did have that.
But it was the love,
And the nurturing that was missing for me.
The lack of love resorted to being rebellious.
Let me act out,
Because no one showed me that it's okay to be angry.
No one would listen,
Or even ask me...
I just did what I was told,
Even if that's not what I wanted.
Maybe if I act out,
They will pay attention.
Maybe they will finally see me,
Maybe they will finally hear me.
Rebellious only triggered them more.
Black and white thinking was all that they knew.
They would threaten me,
Anytime I made a mistake.
Finally,
They made me leave.
This was the extreme,
But to me it was normal.
I felt like I was not part off their team.
Go away, get out of here.
We can't deal,

We want you to leave.
Get out of this house,
Go start a new life.
My mom wouldn't even fight for me.
You can't mess up,
This was all your fault.
Leave your friends,
And your school...
Leave everything that you knew.
The only house you really remember.
Your own mom,
Leave her too.
This message that was sent was what they decided.
Their rules,
Their choice.
They never tried to understand,
What was behind this behavior.
They never tried to connect or fill me up with love.
Just throw me away.
This was just how I felt.
They would tell me,
This is what I deserved.
And this is what was coming.
Because of my behavior,
This was all my fault.
They would never let me forget,
That it was always my fault.
It was me.
It was me, I made the choice.
This was thrown at me,
So many times.
I started to believe it in my own mind.

What this does to a little girl's worth,
Is damaging and it really hurt.
I felt unwanted,
That they gave up.
This created beliefs,
Inside of me.
That I had to hear,
And then set free.
What they would tell me,
Isn't really true.
I was just a little girl,
Crying out for help,
"I need you."
But no one showed me how to actually say that,
Because words were never used,
And love was never shown.
So it was in my behavior,
That is what I turned to.
I was only a kid.
As an adult,
I would believe that everyone was going to leave me.
I need to be perfect,
I need to do everything right.
Can't show my flaws,
Never make a mistake.
Always do good and always succeed.
Failing may bring an extreme consequence.
So just keep putting on that mask,
And create a façade.
That mask will protect you,
And keep you safe.
No one wants to hear you anyways.

My self-worth was shot,
And I didn't even know.
It was when I started taking my mask off...
That's when I saw.
I met this little girl,
And started giving her love.
I would listen and see her.
I would give her what she needs.
I needed to let her know,
It's okay to feel hurt.
I will be here for you,
Whenever you need to cry.
Whatever you need,
You can tell me.
Explain and communicate.
Feel everything you shoved away.
I am here now,
I will keep you safe.
I now know how I should have been treated.
I have found healthier ways.
I now have to listen to that little girl,
And undo that programming.
Create new beliefs.
Taking that mask off,
Taking off all the armor.
I will now allow myself to be seen and heard.
My little girl is so much calmer.

The Scapegoat

Hi! I'm here to have you dump your fears,
And your pain all onto me.
I will take responsibility!
You can project all of your flaws.
Put them on me,
I'll take them all!
Anything you are unhappy with.
Any of your hurt,
That's why you had me.
To take on all of that responsibility.
I will be blamed.
I will be shamed.
And I will never hold you accountable,
Because I've been manipulated into being your slave.
I will put you on a pedestal,
And let you stomp on me.
I'll please you and please you,
And never argue back.
I will stay silent,
As you call me names.
I will take on your labels,
That you've given to me.
I will carry your burdens.
I will meet your needs.
I will do everything to make you happy.
You can yell at me,
And project almost anything.
I'll take it all on.
Carry that load,
Never put it down.

I will let you look perfect,
Keep up that façade.
I will also continue to look perfect,
To protect myself,
Out of fear.
I'll keep everything hidden,
And talk about how great you are.
I will shower you with gifts.
And write letters,
Thanking you for all that you've done.
I'll defend you and praise you,
And make myself small.
I'm grateful for the life that you've given me.
This is what I sincerely believed.
You've conditioned me to act this way.
I was trained and molded to always praise you.
I was conditioned to believe,
That life was this way.
You taught me to sacrifice myself,
And praise you until I had nothing left.
You took it all,
And that was my role.
You put me here.
You loved me here.
You had me just where you wanted me.
All because you didn't want to see...
Any of this in your own self.
You didn't want to deal,
So, throw it at me.
Until one day,
I woke up.
I woke up to this insanity.

I woke up to this emotional abuse.
This life was chaos,
I finally knew.
And I finally saw.
And once I saw,
I could not unsee.
My role as being the scapegoat in this family.
It is over.
My role is ending,
It's time for this exposure.
Manipulation.
Triangulation.
Covert and overt.
Hidden and silent,
It is all now discovered.
I see you.
I see it all,
I see it clear.
I will not go back,
I will disappear.
I will never participate,
In these games again.
No words have been said,
But you know that I know.
Your life is a game,
Of finding the ones,
Who will meet your every need.
A game of conditions,
Power and greed.
Finding the people who will be there,
Guaranteed.
The people who just can't see.

That used to be me.
You can have those people...
I will take myself,
I will leave this game,
And wish you well.

When is it your turn?

Never again will I allow you to be walked on.
Never again will I allow you to be projected on.
I will keep you safe.
I will stand up for you.
I will protect you.
I will validate you.
I will sit with you.
I will love you.
I know that you haven't heard,
The words that you need to hear,
From people that have hurt you.
I know that you haven't been,
Heard or seen.
I know that you have wanted to use your voice.
I know that you have been left,
And taken advantage of.
I know that accountability,
Is important.
I know that acknowledgement,
Is too.
I know that you need to be considered.
I know what you deserve.
When is it your turn?
Your turn is now.
I will make sure of that.
I will make sure that you never feel,
Like you have in the past.
I will take our power back.
I will be assertive.
I will speak up.

I will remove, block, or delete if I am shown disrespect.
You deserve to be heard.
This is absurd.
The way that you have lived.
I finally see it now.
And it is not your fault.
You've been conditioned.
You've been manipulated.
You've been controlled.
You couldn't see.
Just like they can't see now.
It doesn't make it right.
I will tell you now,
Everything you need to hear.
I will show you now,
Everything you need to see.
Your new ways,
Will upset people.
And that is okay.
Empowerment.
Self-love.
It's not about everyone else.
It is about you.
It is your turn now.
Speak your truth.

Fawn

I am sitting face to face with my reality.
That I lived in a trauma response my whole life.
Fawning.
I created this character.
To protect the real me.
This character.
My mask.
This façade.
This character protected me.
Because I was so scared.
I lived in fear.
Looking back,
This way of living was so insincere.
This character was a people pleaser.
She was so nice.
She was funny.
She was entertaining.
Everyone loved her.
What was she so afraid of?
Rejection.
Shaming.
Abandonment.
Love. But with conditions.
Bring this character.
She will be loved.
But only her.
Underneath this façade,
Was this angry little girl.
She became rebellious.
She wanted to fight for herself.

She was a truth teller from the very beginning,
Trying to use her voice.
But anytime she did,
She was shut down.
Rejected.
Or left.
They took her self-worth.
They took what was left.
They took it for them.
She was brought down to distress.
They did not appreciate when she was direct.
She would be punished.
She was never allowed to ever express.
She was only loved,
If they were impressed.
Disagreement was not welcomed.
This is why,
She would fawn.
But she had this mask.
This character protected her.
This character gave her strength.
But underneath it all,
Was this fragile girl.
But this fragile girl,
She finally saw.
She finally figured it out.
She sat up.
She got up.
Enough is enough.
She gave herself love.
She gave herself forgiveness.
It is time to rise above.

This character is gone,
I don't need to fawn.
I need to leave her behind.
Because once I learned
To love myself,
I could leave behind that mask.
I will look in my mirror,
I will look at my face.
I will tell myself,
I am strong.
I am great.
I deserve the best.
I will never settle,
For anything less.
Not ever again.
I am blessed.

Flight

Nurture me, please.
I need you to sit with me.
I need your attention.
Listen to me,
I need to explain.
I need to cry because of all the times,
You've shoved me aside.
Remember when I needed you,
And you went to help someone else?
Remember when I needed you,
And you were trying to fix someone else?
Remember when I needed you,
And you were blaming someone else?
Remember when I called for you,
But you ran away every time?
I needed nurturing and love,
And all you did was run.
Run away.
You ran away.
Your flight response is here.
I understand that you didn't know,
And it wasn't intentional.
You just didn't know,
How could you have known?
It was never taught or shown to you.
So, all you knew,
Was run away.
Run away from me.
I need you now.
Do you hear me?

I need you to
Really understand.
What it means to me
When you stay,
And just hold my hand.
Do you see me now?
Sitting here,
Explaining this
Pain and hurt.
I'm trying to trust you,
After you've shoved me aside.
Sit with me now.
Hear me cry.
Love me now.
Nurture me now.
See me now.
I appreciate this time,
That you've spent,
Trying to learn and understand.
I see how hard it's been,
For you to change your ways.
We're working together now,
You don't have to run.
You've learned to stay.
Stay with me.
You've learned that,
Your flight response isn't helpful at all.
Stay when you want to run.
Love when you want to leave.
Nurture when you just want out.
Running doesn't serve this life.
Because the life you want is

Love.
Love is me.
Love is inside,
Love has been here,
All along.
I am love.
I am here.
I have been here,
All along.
Needing you to stay,
And not run away...
And look for it,
Everywhere else.
Running to love over there,
Then over here.
When it's been inside this whole time.
Thank you for loving me now.
I trust you now,
That you will stay.
Love is me.

The Black Sheep

I am the odd one out.
The one who doesn't fit.
The one who says,
What no one wants to hear.
Let me introduce myself.
I am the black sheep.
I am apparently,
The one,
Who is bad.
And brings shame,
To this family.
The one who doesn't listen.
The one who rebels.
The one who isn't accepted.
The one who is overly emotional.
I am too sensitive.
I am never good enough.
These are all the labels,
That have been given to me.
I am not a real person.
I am just an item.
An item, to make them look good.
An item, that they can use.
Just a tool.
Just a bag,
To throw their shit in.
Sometimes,
I am the ground,
That they stomp on.
Sometimes,

I am the punching bag.
I am the black sheep.
I will never be defended.
I will always be scolded.
I will always be punished,
No matter what.
If I don't conform,
To their every need.
It will be a punishment,
That I receive.
As a kid, but even as an adult.
The black sheep.
The bad one,
Always the bad one.
I will have to act perfect,
Be a person that I'm not.
Be the person they want me to be.
For them to ever acknowledge me.
When they act,
Out of line...
They will never, ever say sorry.
Accountability will never happen,
I accept this.
Because I am the black sheep,
And that is just how it is.
Because I am the black sheep.
I know the role now.
I figured it out.
All of those problems,
That they threw at me.
I can now shrug them off,
It's not my responsibility.

I will no longer be,
The item.
The tool.
The bag.
The ground.
That punching bag.
I will walk away,
Doing the work,
To free myself.
It was them all along.
It was their shit,
On me.
I now know,
How to separate.
Separate myself,
From other people's stuff.
It is not mine,
I will not carry it.
It is not mine,
I will drop it, right away.
It is not mine,
It never was to begin with.
They are all mad...
Because that bag,
Is now closed off.
They have nowhere,
To put all of their shit.
Their emotions.
Their problems.
Their flaws.
Their secrets.
They are all mad,

Because the truth has come out.
The truth sets you free.
You know that saying?
The truth really will set you free.
I am free.
Free from all those years,
Taking on responsibility.
Responsibility, that was never mine.
Never mine,
From the very start.
Being the black sheep,
Was very hard.
But now,
I appreciate,
That "black sheep" in me.
She knows the truth.
She speaks the truth.
She'll never back down.
She'll choose herself.

The Easy One

I am the easy one.
I never speak up.
I go along with what everyone wants.
I do what everyone says.
I please everyone else,
Except for myself.
I won't give my opinion.
I won't speak my truth.
I am known as the easy one.
I am constantly putting you before me.
I am known for going with the flow.
Doing whatever you want.
I just do what's best for you,
Not what's best for me.
I agree when I don't really want to.
I let everything slide.
I let you live your life,
While I rearrange mine.
I rearrange my life,
To fit into yours.
I answer every call.
I respond to every text.
I am always the nice one.
Always the nice girl.
I don't say what's on my mind.
I don't want to rock the boat.
I do it your way,
And keep my mouth shut.
And when I finally open my mouth.
When I finally call you out.

When I am direct.
When I finally speak my truth.
When I start sharing my feelings.
When I change my life so drastically.
When I finally start doing things my way.
When I finally put my foot down.
When I start living the life I choose.
When I finally walk away from abuse.
When I no longer allow you to walk on me.
When I stop agreeing with everything you say.
When I say what I mean.
When I stop telling you what you want to hear.
When I do things for me,
And not just for you.
When I tell you my needs are different now.
When I put my needs first.
When I stop putting in all the effort,
To take care of myself.
When I stop putting up with guilt trips.
When I walk away from one sided relationships.
When I tell you I have changed.
When I am finally honest with myself,
I can start to be honest with everyone else.
When I start being so completely genuine.
When I finally get to be who I really am.
This is when I see,
Who is still standing there at the end.

Done

I am done with the people pleasing.
I am done being told words that aren't genuine.
I am done being manipulated.
I am done with you telling me things you don't mean.
I am done being walked on.
I am done having your words mean nothing.
I am done with you saying things,
Just to keep the peace.
I am done having your actions not match your words.
I am done with you being passive.
I am done trying to figure out what you are saying.
I am done trying to figure out what you mean.
I need you to be honest.
I need you to be real.
I need you to stop sugar coating.
I need you to stop beating around the bush.
Just say what you mean.
Speak the truth.
Be direct.
Say what you have to say.
Just come out with it.
I can't read into what you are trying to say.
That is exhausting.
Exhausting for me.
If you want to say no.
Just say no.
If you don't want to go.
Just don't go.
Decline and move on.

I can't stay stuck,
And figure you out.
Just be your true genuine self.

The Bad One

I was known as the bad one.
She is the bad one.
She is the rebel.
She is trouble.
Whenever I would go out of their control.
Whenever I would do what I was drawn to.
Whenever I would crave freedom.
Runing away from the chaos.
Running away from the control.
Running away from where I didn't want to be.
That is when I was told I was bad.
I was never taught,
I was only punished.
I was never shown,
I was only scolded.
Now that I am an adult,
I need to undo this.
I am an adult.
I can have freedom.
I can do what I want now.
I can find what I love.
And whenever I do this.
You know what I hear?
I hear a million times a day that I am bad.
I am the bad one.
I am trouble.
I was the bad one.
I deserve punishment.
It is time that I undo this,
Because this is not true.

This is a false belief.
Growing up,
I believed this.
It was engrained in my brain.
I heard it all the time.
This rumor went around.
Went around, behind my back.
I became known as the bad one.
I was the bad one.
This limiting belief.
This is what I hear.
This is what I will undo.
I am not bad.
This is not true.
I will work through this wound.
I will work through releasing this belief.
I will create a new belief.
That I deserve freedom.
There was a reason,
I was running.
There was a reason,
I was rebelling.
There was a reason,
I wouldn't listen.
But no one would figure this out.
But they would sit and judge me.
The bad one gets punished.
No one would ask questions.
No one would ask why.
Why is she doing this?
Let's try to figure her out.
It takes two,

Right?
Where is the accountability on the other side?
It's alright,
I will do my work.
This is my job now.
I will figure this out.
But first,
I must not be known as the bad one.
There was a reason for my behavior.
There was a reason.
This reason was rooted.
Rooted deep inside.
Deep inside me,
That I have found.
I have discovered.
I have figured it out.
I will listen.
I will take the time.
I will understand.
I will find empathy.
I will release this belief.
I was never bad.
I just was not shown.
I didn't have the support I needed,
And I didn't know how to say it.
I wasn't really that bad.
I was hurting.
My parents weren't together.
They both found spouses pretty quick.
I wasn't made a priority,
That is just how I felt.
I was brought into homes,

Where I wasn't really wanted.
I lived in homes with silent treatment and control.
Tendencies that were narcissistic.
Alcoholism and Numbing.
Voices were shut down.
I was brought up with fear.
Fear over love.
I didn't feel safe,
So, I shoved down the pain.
If I showed any kind of anger,
I was the one to blame.
Emotions were not accepted.
I was not living in a safe space.
I was treated like an object.
Not like a child.
A sensitive child who felt it all.
Hypervigilance became my sidekick.
How do I need to act?
How do I need to be today?
Stay out of the way.
Don't say a word.
Anything you say,
Will be used against you.
And thrown back in your face.
Living this way became exhausting.
Of course I wanted out.
Of course I wanted fun.
Of course I wanted freedom.
Get out of the control.
Let me run away and have fun.
Can I finally be a kid?
Let me enjoy life.

I really wasn't that bad,
Considering my living conditions.
I was the bad one though,
That's what they say.
That's how I was raised,
Being known as the bad one.
I am taking that back now.
I am not the bad one,
I never was.
Please don't label me with words.
That is not what I needed.
And even after I grew up,
They still called me the bad one.
Always known as the bad one.
The bad one gets punished.
Sorry to say,
Not as an adult now.
I won't be punished.
I will walk away,
Because I am an adult now.
Time to let it go now.
Release this untrue belief.

The Games You Play

I couldn't do anything,
Without you watching.
Without your control,
Without you hacking.
Hacking into the computer,
Invading my privacy.
You watched me like a hawk,
Just to punish me.
You waited and waited,
For me to do something wrong.
You always had a plan,
To throw me under the bus.
Anything to make me look bad,
Even if you had to make it up.
Always playing mind games.
So nice to my face.
But behind my back,
You would turn on me.
Thought nothing of stabbing me.
Stabbing me in the back.
You were the one holding the knife.
The knife that no one could see.
You were out to get me from day one,
You instilled that fear in me.
You were intimidated by me,
From day one.
Why?
Because I was his first love?
Because you never had a sense of self?
Because you didn't love your own self?

You thrived on chaos and drama.
You loved when I was not well.
You loved when I was failing.
You loved to blow me in.
Your favorite thing was punishment.
Your favorite thing was blame.
Your favorite thing is sitting behind a screen.
Whether it was spying on me,
Or pretending to be someone else.
Sending texts that were in your words,
And pinning them on the ones you "love."
Walking around,
Looking like the star.
The star is what you painted.
This picture for everyone to see.
But no one could see.
See,
Who you really are.
No one could see,
Because of your games.
No one could see these games you played.
No one would know this abuse you gave.
You had everyone manipulated,
So that you could be the star.
The winner.
The good one.
The bully,
Is what I saw.
You did it so well.
That if I ever told my story,
None of this would ever make sense.
You will play the victim,

Like you are doing right now.
"Can you believe this is happening to me,"
Your words said by the martyr.
"I would never do such a thing."
Another gaslighting experience from you.
Me over here,
Feeling like I'm crazy.
Trying to piece this together,
Trying to make sense of this.
My brain can't comprehend any of this,
Because I would never act like this.
Oh, it makes sense now.
I see it clear now.
Your games are out in the open now.
I know what is going on.
The difference between me and you,
Is I will walk away.
I don't play games.
The difference between me and you,
You paint the picture,
And I don't need to explain myself.
I know the truth.
I know who I am.
I know what I stand for.
Your true colors will start to leak out.
Your secrets will start to bleed on to others.
Your perfection will slowly start to dissipate,
As you start to lose control.
Because the people who held you up,
Are no longer there.
We're no longer serving you platters,
With pretty words and validation.

We're no longer idolizing you,
Letting you get away with having power.
Walking away.
Away from your games.
I am no longer afraid.
Sending my fear,
Back your way.
You acted this way,
To instill fear in me.
I am giving it back,
It is no longer needed.
Actually, I will send it all back.
All of what you put on me.
All of what I have carried,
I am giving it all back to you now.
I will walk away,
I will leave you with my mask.
My mask I had to put on,
To protect myself from you.
And just hear my words now,
The pain you wanted me to feel...
It is gone now.
I am putting it all down now.
I am doing fine now.
And I will leave you now,
To reveal your true self now.

Knives

Remember that day...
The day you tore me apart.
Tore me apart with your words,
Like a bully.
Remember that phone call?
Do you remember?
Do you remember gaslighting me?
Do you remember not taking any accountability?
Do you remember putting the blame,
All on me?
Do you remember ripping me to shreds,
As you listened to the person sitting next to you?
She was telling you every word to say.
Filling your head,
With words to say.
Painting a picture.
A picture for you.
Do you remember her manipulating you?
Shame on you.
Shame on her.
Do you think I did not know that?
Do you really think,
That was going to go over my head?
Do you really think,
I didn't know what was going on?
Do you remember this day?
Do you remember tearing me down?
Do you remember calling out my flaws...
Using them against me,
As you throw at me...

Throw at me the projections of you.
Everything you are,
You claimed that I was.
Oh...
I won't take that on.
Those are your flaws.
Those are the qualities,
You don't want to see in yourselves.
Do you remember throwing those knives?
Throwing those knives...
Those knives at me?
That you can never take back?
Do you remember that?
Do you remember this attack.
This attack on me.
Did you know that knives leave wounds?
I have never been spoken to.
Spoken to like that.
Those words you spoke,
I know they did not come from you.
They came from someone else,
Who had power over you.
This someone else,
Who was sitting next to you.
That someone else took control.
Took control over you.
Throwing those knives.
But making it look like it is not her.
Pinning the blame,
On anyone but her.
She is not to blame...
She never is.

She is not the one throwing those knives.
She gave those knives to you...
To throw at me.
Those knives were given to you,
So that you can look bad.
You are the bad guy,
It is not her.
How do you not see that?
You just don't know.
It is too late now,
For you to ever see.
Those knives have been thrown at me,
My whole life.
I know these knives well,
And I know who holds them.
I know who throws them.
I know the truth.
I know those words,
That came out of your mouth.
Those words did not come from you.

This Role

This role I played.
This role you know.
This role of the girl,
Who was always okay.
She was always happy,
Always doing fine.
Always put together,
Always on time.
Always there for everyone else.
Always answering every call.
Always saying yes,
Never a mess.
Going out on my worst days,
With a smile on my face.
Being the strong one,
Always the strong one.
Not saying no,
Always on the go.
Doing it all,
Getting everything done.
Everything is perfect,
My life, so put together.
Running around for everyone else.
Fixing everyone's problems,
Not feeling my emotions.
The role I played,
That girl had no emotions.
That girl,
That everyone saw.
That girl,

That everyone knew.
That girl shoved a lot down,
And sacrificed herself.
That girl put up with a lot,
Until she was done.
She cancelled this role.
This role she played,
She stepped out of that lane,
And found her own lane.
Everyone behind her,
Wondering where she went.
Where did she go?
Why is she not fine?
Why is she not smiling?
Why is she not good?
Because I can't be good all the time.
Because I can't play that role.
That role was not who I am.
That role was just a role.
Being good all the time,
Can't even be real.
I can't disappoint anyone,
I will do everything right.
Do what they say,
When they say.
I can't say no,
They are in control.
My role is to stay small,
And walk on eggshells.
Self-sacrifice,
Is not my role anymore.
That role is done.

That role is not me.
It never was,
It was just a role I played.

When I'm Done, I Am Done.

When I'm done, I am done.
No turning back,
No changing my mind.
No turning around,
Things will be different now.
I have a line,
That if it's crossed...
I will take action.
The line that I have,
I've gotten to know.
I've gotten to know it,
Extremely well.
I've gotten to know it,
Many times.
The time that it took,
Me to reach that point...
Used to be longer,
Than it is now.
The reason for this,
Is because I now know my worth.
I believe in myself.
I believe in my truth.
I believe in my heart.
I believe in my soul.
And all of this,
Is part of my worth.
The line that I have now,
Is extremely short.
That line,
If it's crossed,

Will result,
In an action.
This action that I'll take,
Is defending myself.
This action that I'll take,
Will all be for my worth.
This action that I'll take...
Will be because,
I love myself.
Whatever action I take,
Is never to hurt.
The action I take,
It is to honor.
Honor, myself.
The action I take,
Is for that little girl.
That little girl,
Who was never heard or seen.
It will all be for her,
To honor this girl.
To honor her,
Finally.
I've gone so many years,
Dismissing her.
Dismissing her voice,
Dismissing her eyes.
She wanted to speak.
She saw things.
Saw things,
I wasn't ready to see.
She wanted to tell me,
So many times.

This resulted in her screaming,
And my body giving out.
Still,
I kept going.
Still,
I kept doing.
I kept going and going,
Not listening to her.
Until one day,
My line was crossed.
My line was crossed,
One final time.
She forced herself in,
And I finally heard.
This line,
Is her line.
To be honored, adored,
And cared for.
She has deserved this,
All this time.
No more mistreatment,
No more disrespect.
No more being walked on.
No more being used.
This line,
I have.
I am so thankful for.
This line I have,
Is my judgement,
For being done.
I am done with it all.
I am done being mistreated.

I am done with the games.
I am done having this,
Thrown back in my face.
I am done being held responsible,
For things I didn't do.
I am done being responsible,
For a lack of emotional immaturity.
I am done being responsible,
For a lack of self-awareness.
I am done being controlled.
I am done being punished.
I am done being manipulated.
I am done being shamed.
I am done explaining.
I am done fixing.
I am done with attachment.
I am done with toxic.
I am done with projection.
I am done waiting,
For people to change.
I am just done.
These are their problems,
Not mine.
I give them back,
Signed with love.
Love from me.
Love from myself,
That I filled with love.
I welcome the love.
I welcome my people.
I welcome support.
I welcome guidance.

I welcome being seen.
I welcome being heard.
I welcome opinions.
I welcome emotions.
I welcome vulnerability.
I welcome respect.
I welcome partnership.
I welcome real friendship.
I welcome connection.
I welcome anything healthy.
This line that I have.
It is basically saying,
I'm done, when I am done.

Anger

Lashing out.
Reacting.
A short fuse.
Yelling.
Screaming.
Throwing things.
This anger.
This madness.
This chaos.
This violence.
I'll tell you,
It's okay.
It's okay that you're mad.
It's okay to be upset.
It's okay to scream.
Scream and yell.
It's okay.
This anger,
It's okay.
Let me give you this safe space.
This safe space to feel.
Feel your anger.
Unleash this pain.
Regulation.
Regulate this anger.
It must be learned.
Notice.
This anger is here.
Regulate this anger.
It must leave your body.

This anger.
Get it out.
Lashing out.
Yelling.
That burning in your eyes.
Your skin is crawling.
This burst of energy,
Inside of your body.
I am here to tell you,
It's okay.
It's okay that you're angry.
It's okay to feel.
Feel this anger.
Try not to take it out,
On those who love you.
Try not to take it out,
On those you love.
It's hard.
For sure.
We all make mistakes.
Sometimes that anger,
Leaks out.
Leaks out onto our people.
This is when we learn accountability.
This is when we learn apology.
This is when we learn to own our mistakes.
I'm sorry.
I'm sorry goes a long way.
Will you forgive me?
This is when forgiveness comes in.
Anger.
It's not easy to feel.

Anger.
It's easier to shove down.
Anger.
It's easier to blame others.
Anger.
It's easier to just yell.
Find your outlet.
An outlet for this anger.
Anything that works,
Anything that soothes.
Find what helps this anger in you.
Get this out,
Feel it all.
Feel your anger.
It's nothing to be ashamed about.

It Wasn't Until I Left

It wasn't until I left,
That I could see.
See the dysfunction of this family.
It wasn't until I got out,
That it all made sense.
Why I couldn't be myself.
I couldn't be myself,
Inside of that disfunction.
I couldn't be myself,
Around all of that chaos.
I couldn't be myself,
Because I was always put down.
I couldn't be myself,
While they were projecting.
Putting all of their problems,
All onto me.
Using me for their needs.
Throwing the blame,
All over me.
Dimming my light,
That I couldn't even see.
Never taking accountability,
It was always my fault.
Punished and shamed,
And all of the games.
There was no honesty.
Everyone wore masks,
Including me.
No one spoke the truth.
That world was fake.

How could I be myself,
With all of that going on?
I couldn't see,
Until I got out.
I was removed,
So I could see.
See so clearly,
That I didn't belong.
I never belonged.
I never fit in.
It wasn't until I got out,
That it all made sense.
They wanted me to be an extension of them,
But that was never going to happen...
Because I am me.
It wasn't until I got out,
That I could figure out who I wanted to be.
I was finally safe.
Safe to be,
Whoever I wanted to be.
It all came together,
Little by little.
I would never have become aligned,
With them in my life.
I was giving my energy,
To people who stole it.
I was wasting my love,
On people who abused it.
I was putting in effort,
While they put in none.
I was covered in walls,
Just to stay safe.

I hid my true self.
I did not have trust.
I hid my vulnerability.
It was all about them,
And never about me.
I was there for their needs,
While I put mine aside.
I shoved down my feelings,
So, they would be pleased.
And when I finally spoke up,
It was all thrown back in my face.
I thought this was normal,
Until I got out.
Until I got out,
And saw it all.
I finally chose myself,
Over them.
I finally put my foot down,
And defended myself.
I finally called it out.
I said no to the games.
I started to accept,
That they would never change.
This is what they choose.
This is their life.
They can stay there,
While I move away.
Move away from this chaos.
It is peace that I will choose.

Take The Risk

Taking a risk,
Will bring you fear.
Taking a risk,
Will bring you into the unknown.
If you stay,
Where you've always stayed.
If you go,
Where you've always gone.
If you see,
What you've always seen,
You will never get to be,
Who you've always wanted to be.
Take the risk.
Take the leap.
It is in the unknown,
Where you will become,
What you've always wanted to be.
It is in stillness,
That you will hear what is worth facing your fears.
It is in stillness,
That you will discover.
That inner feedback,
That inner knowing.
It is in stillness,
Where you meet your intuition.
Listen.
Your intuition is your calling.
It is in your intuition,
That you will find trust.
You will find trust,

To take that risk.
Your intuition will always guide you.
Just surrender.
It will find you.
Take the risk,
Face your fears.
Trust in your intuition.
Go where you've always wanted to go.
See what you've always wanted to see.
Be who you've always wanted to be.

This Is It

Everyone feels so far away.
Who are you?
Who are they?
Who am I?
I am not who I used to be.
That girl is gone,
But it is her that they see.
I want to scream.
I want to yell.
This process is kind of hell.
I have to keep repeating myself.
No that's not me,
Not anymore.
I don't want to do that.
I don't want to go there.
I have new passions,
I have new likes.
I have new people,
That treat me well.
They just get me,
They just see me.
I don't even have to explain.
Nothing feels the same.
I know it will pass,
I know it's just a phase.
I want out.
I need new.
I keep hearing my calling.
This voice,
That just won't stop.

It gets louder each day.
I have never heard myself,
So clear.
That saying,
"You know when you know."
It couldn't be more true.
I am there now.
I hear it,
Coming through.
It is time.
It's time.
I've been waiting for this.
This is the moment.
This is it.

Someone Else

What do you do,
When you decide to be someone else?
What do you do,
When your old life, just doesn't fit?
What do you do,
When you realize that you're in the wrong place?
I am sitting here,
Asking myself...
Who are you?
And I don't have an answer.
Patience.
It will come.
This is when faith comes in.
Surrender.
This is the moment,
Right for me.
This moment that is here,
Has been here before.
It keeps coming back.
I am listening now.
I am tuned in.
I feel all alone,
In this world.
I feel like it is just me.
I feel like no one sees me,
Or hears me,
When I try to explain.
I am moving towards another self.
I am moving towards who I am supposed to be.
How do I expect people to understand?

It's not about them, though.
This is about me.
Reinvent yourself,
They said.
Be whoever you want to be.
But do they mean that?
Do they mean those words?
Do they understand,
What that really means?
It means leaving everything behind.
It means letting everything go.
That saying,
Life is not easy.
I understand that now.
Growing pains.
Yes, I comprehend that too.
These are the things,
That are not talked about.
These are the things,
People will judge you for.
It's okay,
I'm learning.
It doesn't matter,
I get it.
Never put your worth in someone else's hands.
Right now,
That is really important,
For me to understand.
My worth is in me.
I am worthy.
There will always be,
Someone waiting to take my worth away.

Whatever that is,
Is inside of them,
And has nothing to do with me.
I will ask myself,
Who are you?
And I will respond,
I am me.
I am worthy.
Let everything else,
Come about.
The more I love myself,
The answers will come.
Just keep going,
Never give up.
Change is discomfort.
Discomfort is here.
It's all okay.
One day,
It'll be clear.
I'm in a cocoon,
For now.
Stay here.
It is safe here.
That someone else,
That I will become,
She will appear.
She will leave this cocoon.
She will be free.
She has worked so hard,
To become her.
She has said goodbye,
To everything.

She has sat in so much discomfort.
She cried so many tears.
The day she arrives,
Will be a day of joy.
It will be a day of answers.
I can finally ask,
Who are you?
And answer firmly,
Without a doubt,
Without a care in the world,
I am this girl now.

This Void

A hole.
Black & dark.
Deep & empty.
How do I fill this deep, dark hole?
It will need to be filled,
With love for myself.
Light & love.
Gratitude & strength.
Wisdom & connection.
Nurture this hole.
Value myself.
I am safe.
Safe to fill,
This darkness.
Clear out any distractions.
I am the only one,
Who can do this.
Self-love.
It comes from within...
It comes from seeing every part,
That has been dismissed.
Every part,
That has been unloved.
This void.
This hole.
I can feel it,
Filling up.
I can feel this heaviness,
Leave my soul.
The darkness is replaced with light.

The emptiness is replaced with love.
The weight is replaced with nurture.
This is all because,
I can look at this void.
I see it,
I can hold it.
I embrace it.
I acknowledge that it's there.
No more running away from it.
Let me inside of it.
Let me understand.
I will know what it needs.
I have learned my void.
I know how to listen.
And each time I listen,
There is a release.
A release of pain.
A release of darkness.
A release of the weight,
I have been carrying.
This void has been,
Covering my soul.
My soul has been covered,
All this time.
With each release,
This void gets smaller.
With each release,
I am thankful.
Thankful for finding,
My soul, again.

Just Trying To Figure This Out

Once you find complete worth in yourself,
No one will ever be able to bring you down.
They can say what they want,
They can do what they want.
They can instill fear,
They can play their games.
They can judge you,
And criticize you.
Call you names.
It won't matter,
That can't hurt you.
Say what you want to say.
Talk about my flaws.
Let me keep walking,
I love myself.
That is all that matters.
Nothing externally can affect me now.
The things that you say,
Have more to do with you,
Anyways.
I will send you love,
I will set the tone.
We are all connected.
We are all one.
You might want to look,
At the things that you see in me.
Those might be,
The things you don't want to see in yourself.
Just a thought.
Just some advice.

You don't have to listen.
We don't have to fight.
We are all mirrors,
For each other.
We can all help heal,
One another.
Remove the ego,
And open your heart.
Let the light in,
Love yourself.
This was a lesson,
I had to learn.
Mirrors.
We are all just mirrors.
What I see in you,
Could be...
Something I don't want to see in me.
If something bothers me,
In you,
Let me go inward,
I will check myself.
You are my mirror.
We are all just trying to figure this out.
Figure out life,
Figure ourselves out.
Fighting through the pain,
Finding self-love.
Filling our voids,
And trusting ourselves.
We're all on a journey,
Different paths.
Different ways.

Different speeds.
I am different from you,
You are different from me.
You have your own path,
And I have my own, too.
You focus on yours,
I'll focus on mine.
I used to believe,
It was my job to fix you.
I used to believe,
That was my worth.
I used to believe,
That I had to help,
Everyone other than myself.
I used to sacrifice my own being,
To make others happy,
Or help them along.
I used to not be able to see myself,
At all.
Blame other people,
It was them.
I didn't want to face,
Any of my pain.
I had to find,
Understanding.
That all I am responsible for,
Is myself.
Finding my worth,
Finding my value.
That will be my purpose,
Finding who I am.
Everything will fall into place,

Once I fill that hole,
Inside of my heart.
Once I find wholeness,
And I discover my true self.
I will find forgiveness.
Forgiving my past,
And embracing my future.
Taking steps forward,
No turning back.
Staying on the right track,
Following my heart.

I Won't Be Broken

I can't be broken.
Betray me.
Run me down.
Shut me down.
Stomp on me.
Leave me,
I am still here.
I won't be broken.
I won't be brought down.
I found boundaries.
I found my voice.
I found a power,
Deep within.
I found a love,
That no one can take.
It is mine,
All mine,
And I'm not giving it away.
This love,
That I found,
Will carry me through.
I won't be broken,
It's not going to happen.
I will stand here,
On my own.
I will keep going.
I will rise above,
No matter what.

These Tears Are For You

I have to say goodbye to you.
I have to grieve this girl, I was.
It breaks my heart,
To end our time.
It breaks my heart,
To feel this pain.
It's time to let go.
It's time to switch roles.
I am so sorry.
That your whole life...
You ran around,
For everyone else.
You depended on other people,
To love who you were.
You depended on them,
To see you.
You depended on them,
To hear you.
You never saw it in yourself.
You couldn't see it,
Your vision was blurred.
Blurred by so many distractions,
And roles.
Blurred by expectations,
And love.
Love for everyone,
Except for yourself.
Blurred by a giant hole.
Blurred by your void,
Within.

Blurred by all of this.
The girl that you were,
Is still beautiful to me.
I see you now.
I hear you now.
The fixer in you,
Is who I will grieve.
Your role that you played,
Is who I will mourn.
I will say goodbye,
To that girl with no boundaries.
I will say goodbye,
To that girl with no voice.
Before I could say goodbye to you,
I had to love you.
All of those parts.
You were waiting,
All this time.
For me,
to understand.
Thank you for protecting me.
Thank you for keeping me safe.
So many people around me now,
Keep looking for you.
They all see me, as you.
They're all so confused,
As to where you went.
They don't understand.
They want you back.
I know that you know,
That we can't go back.
I know that you know,

That I deserve this new path.
I know that you know,
This is what's best.
But that doesn't make it,
Any easier.
The pain that I have,
In my heart.
Is a pain that I feel,
It is so sharp.
Letting go of everything else,
Has been so hard.
But the hardest thing,
Is saying goodbye to you.
You are my girl.
You are my rock.
You have been screaming,
All of these years.
How do I leave you now?
How do I say goodbye to you?
You have been here all along.
You are so loved.
You are beautiful,
Every single part of you.
I can bring you along,
I just can't have you lead.
I don't need you anymore,
You have taught me so much.
You have given me,
This strength inside.
You have given me,
The power to lead.
These tears,

Are for you.
Goodbye, to you.
Hello, to me.

The Ego

The things that I am saying,
Are affecting you.
The things that I am *not* saying,
Are affecting you.
The things that I say,
Are bringing you discomfort.
The things that,
I *don't* say,
Are bringing you internal struggle.
It is not,
What I am saying.
It is not,
What I am *not* saying.
It is something in you,
That needs to be healed.
That you,
That's inside.
Is calling out.
This discomfort is you,
Needing something.
Needing something,
From you.
And you are the only one,
Who can figure that out.
It is not my job,
To make you feel comfortable.
It is not my job,
To cater to your feelings.
I don't mean any harm,
By the things that I say.

Your ego,
Is here.
To protect you.
Protect you from feeling,
Any kind of pain.
Protect you from looking,
At your own self.
Protecting you,
From what's inside.
Your ego is what points the finger.
Your ego wants to find blame.
Your ego is what manipulates.
Your ego is what finds addiction.
Your ego is what needs validation.
Your ego is what doesn't want to hear this.
Your ego,
Is the anger,
That lashes out at what I say.
Your ego wants you to believe,
That I am the one bothering you.
Your ego wants,
What it wants.
Your ego is the control.
Your ego, is why you're upset.
It is your ego, that is judging me.
It is your ego, that wants to put me down.
If it wasn't for your ego,
You could shrug off my words.
What's underneath your ego?
That's who you really are.
Do you have a self,
Underneath that ego?

Who is it?
It is pure love.
We are all just pure love,
Underneath our egos.
Underneath all of our pain.
Who are you?
Who are you, really?
Heal.
Face the pain.
Face that internal struggle.
Face that discomfort.
You will have to fight that ego off.
You will have to fight, so many times.
You will have to understand,
That ego.
You will have to understand,
That is not who you are.
You will have to stop reacting,
Against that ego.
You will have to stop,
Allowing,
That ego to control you.
You will have to fight that off,
So many times.
You have to start,
Pausing.
That's when you change.
That's where that growth is.
It is in the pause.
Once you figure it out,
You will see.
The words that I am saying,

They are not to hurt you.
They are just,
Me.
Speaking my truth.
And, that is all.

Putting Herself Back Together Again

She's been putting herself,
Back together again.
It seems that she's done this,
A thousand times.
She's been replacing,
Piece by piece.
She's been reflecting,
And constructing.
She's been rebuilding,
And repairing.
She's been reprogramming,
And listening.
She's been releasing,
And letting go.
She's been feeling,
So that she can heal.
She's been putting herself,
Back together again.
She's put together,
This whole new self.
She's put her together,
Through all the pain.
She's put her together,
Through this turmoil.
She's put her together,
Piece by piece...
So that she can feel whole.
So that she can feel whole,
All by herself.
Instead of looking

For it somewhere else.
She's put her together,
In this place.
This place,
This land,
That she's grown up in.
This place,
She's never left.
This place,
Is all she's known.
This place,
Is a reminder to her,
Of all the times that she's been burned.
This place no longer is fulfillment to her.
This place has been a piece,
That she's been needing to release.
It was a place,
That she once loved.
It was a place,
That filled her heart.
It was a place,
That made her smile.
It was a place,
She felt connected to.
It used to be her happy place.
But now this place,
Is a reflection of,
All the hurt that she's endured.
This place used to mean the world to her,
And now that's been taken away.
She has been put back together again,
In this place.

And she now realizes that,
This place will never feel the same.
It will never feel,
As it once did.
It will never fulfil her heart again.
Not how it used to,
Not how it was.
This place was a part of her old self.
This place was a part of her broken heart.
This place was a part of her old role.
This place was a part of her old life.
This place was no longer for her,
She could feel it,
Deep within.
She now realizes,
That she needs a new place.
A new place for her to start.
A new place for her to excel.
A new place for her to grow.
A new place for her to spread her love.
A new place for her to be.
A new place for her to feel fulfilled.
This will be her place.
This will be her happy place.
A place just for her.
For her new self.
A place that she has prepared to go.
A place that she has seen in her dreams.
A place that will allow her to be,
Whoever she wants to be.
A place that won't be a reminder to her,
Of all the times...

She had to put herself back together again.
A place that won't be a reminder to her,
Of all the pain she's felt.
This place,
Still has beautiful people,
That mean the world to her.
They are all in her new heart.
She has made sure to put them there.
She's made sure to make a place for them.
They will always be there,
In her new heart.
That will never change,
that will go with her.
This new place,
Is her new start.
This new place,
Is for her new heart,
That she put back together.
She put it back together,
Through so many tears.
Through so much emotion.
So much letting go.
She now believes,
In her whole heart,
That this new place,
Is where her destiny starts.

Vulnerability

Be who you are.
Be seen.
Be heard.
Share.
Connect.
Take the risk.
Share your feelings,
Be true to you.
You're exposed now.
You risk being wounded.
You risk being left.
You risk being judged.
You risk being criticized.
But what are you risking?
Not being accepted?
Not being yourself?
Not being accepted for who you really are?
What are you risking?
People talking about you?
Losing a relationship?
Are they really your friend,
If they don't accept your words?
Are you worried that you will rock the boat?
Make them mad?
Make them upset?
Vulnerability is honest.
Vulnerability is raw.
Vulnerability is naked.
It's when you come out of hiding.
It's when you honor your true self.

Vulnerability is not about approval.
It's not about pleasing.
It's truly about showing up,
For your true self.
Showing up for others.
Showing up in the world.
Vulnerability will lead to connection.
Vulnerability will lead to your true people.
Being vulnerable is a muscle.
The more you use it,
The easier it is to show up.
It is a practice.
It will bring intimacy.
It will bring discomfort.
It will bring big feelings.
It might bring disappointment.
It might bring change.
People may leave,
Once you start to be real.
People may get defensive,
If they don't like what you're saying.
People may shut down,
When you start to feel.
When you open up,
And speak the truth.
Some won't like what you have to say.
They will decide what is best for them...
What is best for them,
May be to leave.
People leaving,
May lead to grief.
Grief, for you.

For you, To feel.
Vulnerability can be dangerous.
Dangerous,
To those who want to hide.
They may have to leave.
Because they just can't deal.
It makes them truly uncomfortable,
And that's okay.
That's their choice.
Let them leave.
Let them go.
Let them be.
Because what is the point,
If you can't be yourself?
What is the point,
If you can't be honest,
And share?
Share what's in your heart.
Share the hard things.
Vulnerability can be dangerous,
Because it is full exposure.
Exposure to the one,
Who is raw.
Exposing your honest, true self...
Is not an easy journey.
It can be a bumpy road.
But it is the only way,
To be authentic.
Authentic people will find,
The others.
The others, who are risking,
Being authentic as well.

Being authentic will lead to connection.
Connection is a true gift.
A gift of love.
A gift of risk.
A gift of showing up.
Vulnerability is brave,
It's naked and raw.
Vulnerability is beautiful.
Vulnerability is everything.
Everything, coming out.
Let it out,
It's time to be seen.
It's time to just be you.
And set yourself free.

What Are You Saying?

What are you saying?
I don't understand.
Can you be more specific?
This is getting out of hand.
Why am I always trying to figure out,
What people mean?
Just say what it is.
Whatever you're trying to say.
What does that mean?
Is that a question?
I guess?
That might work?
Maybe?
Does this mean that you're passive?
Silence.
Sighing.
Pouting and Moodiness.
Excuses and sarcasm.
Are you being passive aggressive with me?
What is this communication?
I just don't understand.
Is this a game that you're playing?
Can you be more direct?
I'm not going to chase you down.
I'm not going to figure this out.
It is not my job,
To figure out these behaviors.
It is not my job,
To figure out what you mean.
Figure out your needs,

And then express them.
Figure out those feelings,
And express those too.
Figure out direct communication,
Leave behind those passive behaviors.
Your life will get so much easier.
Be assertive.
Be direct.
Put it out there.
It's okay.
What are you afraid of?
Remember,
Freedom of speech.
That used to be me,
That passivity.
That passive aggressive way.
Not being clear,
Not being direct.
I had to learn.
Learn it for myself.
Learn it for others.
It wasn't easy.
I had to find my worth, first.
I had to love myself.
I had to move through the fear.
Fear of not being accepted,
For something that I said.
Fear of not being liked.
Fear of being judged.
Fear of being punished.
I had to get to know myself.
So that I could clearly express.

Express my needs and feelings.
Express who I really am.
Communication came,
Once I found love for myself.
I could communicate directly now,
Because I became clear on me.
Clear on my needs.
Clear on my wants.
Clear on my feelings.
Clear on my people.
Find the people who hold space for you.
Find the people who hear you.
Find the people who give you space.
Find the people who let you be.
Those are the people,
That allow you to speak,
However, you want to speak.
Those are the people,
Who accept,
Freedom of speech.
Be direct,
Just say whatever it is.
Say the words,
That align.
The words that align,
With who you are.
The words that align,
With what you're trying to say.
The words that align,
With your soul.
Words are important.
Let them be genuine.

Find the words,
That you want to say.
Be direct.
Be clear.
It is so much easier...
When you don't have to guess,
What that gesture means.
It is so much easier...
When you don't have to guess,
What does that phrase mean?
It is so much easier...
When you don't have to people please.
People pleasing is a form of communication.
Communication to be liked.
Communication to be accepted.
Communication to fit in.
Communication, that is passive.
Passive brings confusion.
Direct brings clarity.
Just be clear.
Use your words.
Your words aren't meant to be liked.
Your words aren't meant to make others feel good.
Your words can be uncomfortable.
Your words can be truthful.
Your words can be assertive.
Your words are specifically,
Meant to communicate.
Let your words align with you.
Let your words just be words.

Tears

Tears.
So many tears.
So much sadness.
So much grief.
So much loss.
So much pain.
So many tears,
Are coming again.
So much release.
So much letting go.
Let that old self go,
Let your soul show.
Let those expectations go.
Let those limiting beliefs go.
Let those negative emotions leave.
Let those tears,
Flow down your face.
Feel all those sensations.
Feel it all,
It's not here to stay.
Feelings come.
And feelings go.
Sensations will be.
And then they will leave.
That knot in your throat,
Tune in.
It can be released.
That knot is pain,
Waiting to leave.
That sharp shooting pain,

In your stomach.
That is radiating pain,
That can't wait to go.
Your body is doing all of this work.
This is what your body,
Is made for.
Healing.
Have faith.
Have faith in these tears.
Doctors will diagnose depression.
They'll diagnose bipolar.
They'll say something is certainly wrong with you.
You shouldn't be feeling so bad,
All the time.
Humans should only be happy.
Walk around with a smile.
Sleep should be steady.
You should just act "normal".
Emotional pain,
Is not accepted.
Emotional turmoil,
Is looked down on.
Emotional sensations.
And internal struggle.
This is what society will judge you for.
These emotional sensations,
If not released...
These are the sensations that manifest,
Physically.
But now,
The doctors will hear you.
Now,

The doctors pay attention.
Now,
That there's a medical condition to treat.
This is our system.
Our system doesn't make room for tears.
Take your tears,
And medicate them.
Take your tears,
And suppress them away.
Take your tears,
And shove them inside.
Take your tears,
You are seriously depressed.
These labels,
That are given.
Label it,
And fix it.
These tears.
They signify,
To me…
My journey.
These tears,
Are every feeling I've had.
Leaving my body.
Leaving my soul.
These tears,
Are my awakening.
These tears,
Are setting my soul free.
These tears.
My tears.
They are just tears.

They do not need a label.
They just need love.
Be gentle with your tears.
They are your soul,
Coming to life.
Your body knows just what to do.
Your body knows how to uncover your soul.
These tears,
Are an unveiling.
These tears,
Are a lifting...
Of the pain that you've been holding.
These tears,
Are your soul's red carpet.
Let your tears be.
Let your tears flow.
Love your tears.
They are all for your soul.

Inspired

I want to feel inspired,
By what is around me.
Feel inspired.
Feel it all around me.
Feel inspired.
Feel the drive.
Striving to be better.
Striving for growth.
Change is good.
Learning, a must.
Vulnerability,
I love.
Genuine,
Yes.
I can't be fake,
Not anymore.
Be there for everyone else,
Except for myself.
When I needed quiet,
I didn't say so.
When I needed care,
I ran away.
Ran away to any distraction,
That would keep me from hearing myself.
That is what I knew.
And when I was real…
I was shut down,
Scolded,
Or ran away from.
That's okay.

I understand.
That wasn't about me.
I finally understand that now.
I put myself aside,
For far too long.
Take care of myself now.
Take care of me.
I chose productivity,
Over creativity.
Being productive,
Is how I ran away.
Ran away from myself.
My productivity kept me,
From my creativity.
Productivity was my distraction.
Distraction from inspiration.
Distract myself.
Hurry, don't feel.
Distract myself,
From anything that's real.
Distract myself,
From the pain.
Finally, I chose a new path.
I took the path of,
Inspiration.
Open my mind.
Learn from you.
Inspired by you.
Inspired by me now.
The way you carry yourself,
It affects me.
The way you are living,

It is impactful.
We are what we surround ourselves in.
Your open mind.
It inspires me.
The way you choose to be.
It is motivating.
The way you own your flaws.
That vulnerability.
I want inspiration.
I will follow that.
I appreciate your efforts,
That you put into yourself.
I have learned from you.
I have learned on this path.
You inspire me.
I feel inspired now.

Passion

That passion.
What is your passion?
What do you love?
What lights you up?
Your passion.
It is in your heart.
You move along,
Carrying it within you.
Your passion.
Your interests.
Your ignition.
It ignites a power,
Deep within you.
It ignites your drive.
It ignites your soul.
You crave more.
Crave more passion.
Your passion is your light.
Your passion is you.
Bring your passion,
Alongside you in life.
This passion is important.
This passion will serve you.
This passion will serve others.
This passion is your battery.
This passion is your battery,
For love and joy.
As long as you have your passion,
You are good.
Keep your passion,

Hold it close.
Keep your passion,
Fill your soul.
Your passion is your light.
Your passion is you.
Carry it.
Bring it.
Give it.
Love it.

Surrender

Grieving what was.
Grieving what you won't have.
Grieving what you pictured.
Grieving what you thought your life would be.
Grieving those thoughts you painted,
In your head.
Grieving a future,
That is not aligned for you.
Grieving a plan,
That your mind made.
Grieving your old self,
That is not here anymore.
Grieve it all.
Let it go.
Grieve.
Grieve.
Grieve.
It's time for surrender.
Just let it be.
No more plan.
No more painting a picture.
Trust and let go.
It is only, surrender.
Surrender and accept.
Accept what is.
What is in this moment.
This moment is here.
Forget the "should be".
Forget the "will be".
Forget the "this is how it's supposed to be."

This moment.
It just is.
Accept it for what it is.
Accept this life, for how it really is.
Accept reality.
Accept all of it.
This is what life is.
This is where you are.
The thing with a plan,
Is you can't control it.
The thing with wanting life,
A certain way.
You can't control that either.
We can't control a situation.
We can't control people.
We can't control anything, really.
We just have to let it be.
Let go of that part.
The part of you,
That wants to control.
Let go of that girl,
Who wants to paint that picture.
Let go of her.
This new girl,
That you are becoming.
She will just surrender.
She won't have a plan.
She will just live for the moment.
She will just trust.
Trust what's meant to be.
Trust in a future,
That is in God's hands.

Trust in a future,
That she can't control.
Trust in a future,
That is for her.
A future,
That is for her...
That she can't predict.
She can't predict,
What is coming.
She can't predict,
What will happen.
She can't predict,
Her future.
She'll leave her control.
She'll leave it behind.
She'll just be.
She'll just live.
She'll just be in the moment.
The moment that's here.
The moment that's now.
She'll just be present.
She'll grieve what was.
She'll grieve that plan.
She'll grieve what she wanted.
And then she'll just be.
She'll just be whatever she's supposed to be.
This moment that comes,
She'll take for what it is.
She knows what she wants,
But she'll accept what is given.
She'll accept her life,
For what it is.

She'll accept it all,
And then she'll be grateful.
Grateful that she surrendered her control.

What Is Now?

What is next?
Who knows.
What is to come?
That can't be answered.
Why are you thinking of what is next?
What is next,
Is a future thought.
What is next,
Is not in this moment.
What is next,
Is not important.
What is now?
That's the question.
This moment, now.
Right now.
Be in it.
Right now.
Own it.
It's all we really have.
This very moment.
Not the next.
We can't control that next moment.
Just be here.
Be here now.
Be in this moment.
Right now.
Let go of everything else.
And just be here.
This is where I love to be.
This is where my life is.

I will accept myself here.
Here in this moment.
Here, right now.
I will accept that this is my life.
This is my life,
Right now, in this moment.
What is next?
It will come.
I will wait,
And it will come.
The next moment,
Whatever it's supposed to be.
Whatever is for me,
Is what is next.
Just trust in what's next.
Trusting and surrender.
What's next will come.
For now,
Be here.
I am here now.
I will be here,
Right now.
This is what I have.
What is now?
That is the question.

This.

Familiarity.
The known.
Comfortable.
The same.
Those are words,
I am leaving behind.
I don't need familiar.
I can embrace the unknown.
I crave to be uncomfortable.
I need different.
This change.
This new life.
New ways.
New eyes.
New words.
New people.
Everything new.
Nothing the same.
Please bring me different.
Bring in the unknown.
I am ready.
Ready for this.
Ready for new.
Ready for change.
I am ready for new beliefs.
I am ready for new challenges.
I am ready for new values.
I am ready to walk a new path.
I will not continue,
The same way I have.

I will not continue,
On the same path.
I will make a U-turn.
This turn,
Onto a bumpy road.
Some ditches.
And some hills.
It's all okay.
I've got this.
I've gotten to know my fear very well.
I've gotten to feel it,
And then let it go.
I know how to walk,
Side by side.
Side by side with my fear.
It can be right next to me.
I will embrace it,
I know what it is.
I am okay with it being here.
I won't run away.
Run away from it.
We are friends now,
Me with this fear.
That was me.
Me, before.
Before this new path.
That showed me new light.
This new light,
Has brought the faith.
It's brought the trust.
It's made me brave.
Let's go.

Walk ahead.
Steps forward.
Chin up.
Keep going.
Embrace.
That uncomfortable is here.
Step right into,
That unknown.
Nothing will be familiar,
Not anymore.
This is what I asked for.
This is what I've been waiting for.
This.

Flow Of Life

Take the leap.
Take the plunge.
Take that road,
You belong on.
Go with your gut.
Go with that feeling.
Listen to your intuitive guide.
Are you listening?
Are you really paying attention?
Are you waiting for that sensation?
Are you ready?
Ready for what?
Ready for what's waiting for you.
Ready for what's in front of you.
You have worked really hard.
You deserve this.
You know you do.
Your heart is yours.
All yours.
Follow your heart.
You've given up your control.
You have learned surrender.
Surrender to you.
Surrender to your dream.
Leave your old life.
Leave it behind.
You know you don't fit.
You feel it,
Every minute.
You know your strength.

Go with it.
Take the leap.
Go with the flow.
The flow of life.
The flow of life,
It's your calling.
Your calling will take time.
It won't be immediate.
Take the plunge.
Trust in yourself.
You belong,
Someplace else.
This feeling,
Is bittersweet.
The grief you feel.
The excitement of what's ahead.
Disconnection.
Disconnect.
Signs are everywhere.
Pay attention.
Follow your signs.
Ask for them.
The signs will show you,
When the time is here.
It's not here now.
It's not here yet.
The time is not now.
You will know when it's time.
Right now,
The process of disconnection.
Right now,
The grief.

Right now,
Feel.
Right now,
Prepare.
Right now,
Enjoy.
Right now,
Be grateful.
Take the leap.
The choice is yours.
Yours.
All yours.
Follow your heart.
Follow the flow of life.

Inside World

Inside.
Inside, I just don't connect to my outside world.
Not anymore.
Not like I once did.
I once was connected.
Connected to what was outside of me.
Connected to my world,
The only world I knew.
What happened?
How did I get here?
What is this shift?
Why can't I get to where I once was?
It is growth.
But it is more than just growth.
It is a transformation.
An internal shift.
This shift,
Inside of me.
It's happening each day.
Each day,
I feel further and further away.
Further away,
From this outside world.
Further from the world,
That I have built.
It's not that I don't enjoy it.
It's not that I don't love it.
I love this world.
I love these people.
That is what is so hard to face.

I've never felt like this.
Felt like this before.
This is new.
I don't know how to navigate.
I don't know how to explain.
This inside shift.
This inside world.
My inside world,
It is all new.
A world,
I'm getting to know.
A world,
That only I know.
My insides.
No one can see.
No one can understand.
No one, but me.
It is really beautiful here.
I will admit.
But scary too,
Because I just don't fit.
I don't fit,
Not anymore.
I don't fit,
Into that outside world.
That outside world,
The one that I know.
I'm so far away.
So far away from it.
This awakening.
I am awake.
Awake to this shift.

Awake to this change.
Awake to the disconnect.
Awake to this world.
I am awake to this new inside world.
I am aware.
I am aware,
Of everything.
All of it.
I feel confused.
It is so different.
I feel so disconnected,
From the outside world.
But I've never felt more connected,
To myself before.
I am so connected.
I am so aware.
I love myself,
Like I never have before.
Maybe this is what wholeness feels like.
Maybe this wholeness,
Needs a new place.
This experience,
I can't even explain.
This doesn't make sense.
Make sense to me.
So how do you make sense of it?
My insides.
They are new.
All new.
My insides.
They don't match that outside world.
This realization.

It's pretty intense.
I feel like I am an alien.
On another planet.
This new planet,
Just for me.
What is this feeling?
The only way I can explain,
Is...
My insides are different.

Wide Awake

Wide awake.
Ideas and thoughts.
So many ideas.
Ideas,
That I have.
My creativity is so alive.
Alive in me,
It just won't stop.
These ideas,
I'm letting them come.
I let them come,
I let them pass.
These ideas.
Ideas I have.
These ideas,
They'll need an action.
Action,
That I'm not prepared to take.
Not right now.
I'm not there yet.
Right now,
I just want to be.
I just want to be,
And not do anything.
I'm trying to work on,
That part of me.
The part of me,
That needs to do.
That part of me,
That needs to accomplish.

Accomplish to feel,
Like I am worthy.
That part of me,
That needs to succeed.
That part of me,
That needs to pick something.
Pick something now.
Hurry.
The rush.
That part of me,
Can learn to relax.
I am teaching myself.
To pause and wait.
Pause and wait,
There is no rush.
What's meant to be,
Will be.
What's meant to come,
Will come.
There is a plan.
A plan for me.
I don't need to jump,
With full force.
Whatever my plan is,
Will be there for me.
Whatever is waiting,
It is here for me.
Here for me,
Whenever it's time.
These ideas that come,
I'll let them be.
They are here,

For when I am ready.
I don't have to do anything.
Not right now.
I can just enjoy.
Enjoy life.
Enjoy myself.
Enjoy me.
Accept what this life,
Has brought to me.
I will make the move,
When it is time.
I will take an action,
When I am there.
For now,
Enjoy.
Being wide awake.
See it all.
Hear it all.
Take it all in.
Relax and just be.
Be in my own creativity.
Be wide awake.
I am not asleep.
I am wide awake.
I am so conscious.
So aware.
So awake.
Pause and be.
Wait and see.
Disappear,
Into this world.
This world of consciousness.

Wide awake,
Through all the layers.
Wide awake,
Just enjoy it here.
Why look for something better?
Just be happy here.
For now,
Enjoy all the ideas.
For now,
Just be.
Just be,
Wide awake.

Cocoon

Something doesn't always have to happen.
Sometimes,
What is happening is nothing.
Sometimes,
What is happening is a recharge.
Sometimes,
What is happening is a rebirth.
Sometimes,
What is happening is a break.
A break from it all.
A break from reality.
A break from accomplishing.
A break from doing.
A break from the world.
A break for you.
A break is okay.
A break is good.
A break is breathing room.
A break is self-care.
A break from the storms.
A break from the work.
The work that you are doing on yourself.
This work is showing.
It's showing in you.
It's showing.
It's rewarding.
And that deserves a break.
A break from something happening.
A break from the next step.
A break from what comes next.

A break from your calling.
A break from your future.
This is a cocoon.
The cocoon you have made.
The cocoon that you're in.
This cocoon is your break.
This rebirth.
That is what is happening.
It is happening inside of this cocoon.
How long in here?
However long you need.
This is your rebirth.
There is no time frame.
This cocoon is safe.
This cocoon is your growth.
Growth in silence.
Growth in peace.
Growth in stillness.
There is actually a lot that is happening.
Happening in here.
Happening in this cocoon.
You are alive and well.
You are filled with love.
You are preparing for your breakthrough.
You are preparing for your exit.
There is no time frame,
Don't forget that.
There is no rush.
There is only peace.
There is only calm and serenity,
Inside of this cocoon.
This stillness is your action.

This stillness,
Is your something happening.
This cocoon you've made.
It's all yours.
It's all yours,
Until you leave.

Hold On

Hold on.
Hold on for this ride.
You are along for the ride.
The ride of healing.
The ride of emotions.
The ride of emerging,
Into your true self.
The ride of revealing,
This work that you've done.
The ride of digging deep.
Deep inside of yourself.
Deep within,
Your layers you've held.
These layers are emotions.
Emotions you've shoved away.
Shoved away for such a long time.
Shoved away,
So that you didn't have to feel.
Shoved away,
So that you didn't have to see.
Shoved away.
Just shove it away.
Just don't go there.
Just don't pull it out.
Just keep moving.
Moving forward.
Just keep moving,
Until it all comes out.
It will come out.
Somehow.

Someway.
These layers make their way up.
No more ignoring.
No more shoving it down.
It's time to face these demons.
These demons,
You've held.
Hold on.
Hold on,
This ride that you're on.
It's up and it's down.
It is tumultuous.
It is unknown.
It is new territory.
Hold on for this ride.
This ride of healing.
Emotions will come.
Ready to start feeling?
No more numbing.
No more running away.
You've committed now,
To go on this ride.
This ride of healing.
It really is rewarding.
The peace that will be there waiting.
That peace,
Is nothing like you've felt before.
Serenity and love,
More rewards.
Alignment and higher vibrations,
Will be at the end.
This ride is worth it.

Don't give up.
Cry those tears.
Feel that fear.
Let out that anger.
Admit your shame.
Your guilt will come out.
Your voice will come.
Your eyes will open.
The mask comes off.
No more hiding.
The illusion is gone.
What's left is,
This reality.
Reality of life.
Reality of what is now.
Let go of the plan.
Let go of the pain.
Let go of the control.
Let go of your ego.
Get rid of it all.
You don't need it.
You're on this ride.
This ride of healing.
Hold on.
But not too tight.
Learning to let go.
Let go when you need to.
Letting go is dangerous.
Because once you've lost it all,
You become unstoppable.
You can't stop,
Not now.

You've endured so much.
You're on this ride.
Hold on,
But not too tight.

Shedding

I am shedding what was.
I am shedding what was supposed to be.
I am shedding off old layers.
I am shedding what doesn't serve me.
I am shedding what doesn't work.
I am shedding parts of me.
I am shedding old behaviors.
I am shedding old feelings.
I am shedding who I used to be.
I am shedding words I used to say.
I am shedding it all.
This doesn't serve me,
Not anymore.
Why did I used to do things,
That I didn't want to do?
Why didn't I speak up,
When I wanted to?
Just be free.
Just shed.
Shed it all.
Keep going.
Find it all.
What doesn't work.
Shrug it away,
And shed it off.
This isn't good for me.
Either is that.
This doesn't make me happy.
And either does this.
This is not me,

Not anymore.
This is old me.
This is how I used to be.
No,
This isn't it.
Either is this.
Keep on moving,
Until I find what I love.
Keep on moving,
Until I find what works.
Keep stepping forward,
Until I am content.
Shed this.
Shed that.
Shed this too.
I am shedding away.
No wonder I don't know who I am.
No wonder I am confused.
No wonder I feel like I am new.
No wonder I feel like,
I haven't been here before.
Right.
Because I haven't.
I have this new skin.
I have shed away,
All of the old.
I have shed away,
Everything I knew.
All of what I knew,
It isn't here anymore.
Shed my old ways,
Find new ways.

I am free.
Free from the old.
Free from what was holding me back.
Free from the weight,
I was carrying.
This shedding.
This release.
Get this off.
Off of me.
I don't need it.
Not anymore.
I can't use it.
I won't do it.
Just keep shedding.
There is more.
This, I can't do.
This, I'm not carrying.
This, I'm dropping.
This, is not mine.
This, is hers.
Why is it on me?
Why did I take this on?
Shed this off.
This disrespect,
Yeah.
Not working.
Shed that off.
Walk away.
This manipulation,
Yeah.
Not okay,
Shedding this too.

Not working for me.
This new skin.
It only has room,
For authenticity.
This is me.
This new skin.
I will shed,
Where do I begin?
Oh, I found more.
Here is this,
Not mine.
What is this?
Why is this on me?
That used to be me?
I used to do that?
I used to say that?
Get it off.
Shedding that too.
There's more?
This,
Nasty behavior?
I only have room,
For kindness and compassion.
I will empathize with you,
And send you love from a distance.
Walking away.
Shedding that as well.
Oh, these games?
These games that you play?
Shedding those too.
I won't play a game.
I'm walking away.
I can't be talked down to.

I will shed that too.
This shedding.
Oh,
It's so free.
I feel so light.
What took me so long?
These expectations,
Put on me,
From society.
I don't need those.
Toss that away too.
The only person,
I'll answer to now,
Is me.
This shedding,
Hasn't been easy.
This shedding brings grief.
This shedding can bring heartbreak.
This shedding is leaving all that I knew.
All because,
I couldn't live there anymore.
I couldn't be that girl,
Not anymore.
This shedding,
Meant losing what I love.
All to make room.
Make room for me.
Make room for my authenticity.
This shedding.
This process.
Led me to this.
Finding myself.
Finding me.

Holding Space

It is how you show up.
It is how you hold space.
It is about being present.
Listen fully.
Listen completely.
It is about putting this person,
As the center.
The center is for them,
And their words.
The center is for them,
And their emotions.
I will give you empathy.
I will give you silence.
I will feel you out,
Whatever you need.
I am not here to fix.
I am not here to make you better.
I am here to love.
Give my love.
Let me just hold space.
Hold space for you.
I will listen.
Listen,
Without judgement.
I will listen,
Without advice.
I will listen,
Without inserting myself.
Holding space.
Just showing up.

I will show up for your experience.
Give you my time.
Give you my energy.
Just be there to listen,
And nothing more.
Let you cry.
Let you feel your emotions.
Create a safe space,
So, you can be completely open.
I can ask you questions.
I can just stay silent.
I can help you process,
If that's what you need.
I can give you my empathy.
I want you to feel seen.
I want you to feel heard.
I want you to feel safe.
I want you to understand,
You can just be.
Be here now.
Be present.
Whatever you need,
In this moment.
This space.
This space is for you.
I will hold space.
Hold space,
For you.
Your struggles are hard.
Your emotions are real.
You just have to feel,
Feel it all.

You don't have to do it,
All alone.
It is so nice to feel understood.
It is so nice to feel seen.
Holding space.
It is so important.
It is a place for full vulnerability.
Share.
Share it all.
Feel what you have to feel.
Be completely real.
This space for you,
It is a no judgement zone.
It is not for pity.
It is not for gossip.
This space,
I hold.
It's for your soul.

Settle

Settle for a life that is for you.
Settle for a life that is yours.
Settle for the right path.
Settle for what your soul says.
Settle for what is meant for you.
Never settle for anything less.
Don't settle for less.
Less than what you deserve.
Don't settle for a life,
That just isn't yours.
Don't settle for people,
Who don't treat you right.
Don't settle for what brings you down.
Don't settle for,
What is not for you.
You must keep going,
Until you find your life.
The life that you want.
The life that you crave.
Efforts that match yours.
Behaviors that make you feel good.
Conversations that are supportive.
Responses that are uplifting.
People who challenge you.
People who inspire you.
People who understand you.
Those people that just see you.
Settle for those people.
Settle into that.
The life that is for you.

It will feel good.
It will feel light.
It will be easy,
Never a fight.
You won't have to explain.
You won't have to defend.
Sometimes,
Words may not even have to be said.
You can just relax.
You can just be.
You can figure yourself out.
Figure out where you need to be.
Go wherever you need to go.
So you can be yourself.
Be you.
Just be.
Be who you are meant to be.
The right people will be there,
Standing at the end.
Cheering you on.
Supporting you.
They want what's best for you.
Settle for that life.
Settle for this.
Settle for everything,
That supports who you are.
Settle for love.
Love that just is.
Love that feels good.
Love that does not hurt.
Settle for that.
Settle for this life.

Sometimes,
Finding that life,
Means leaving another.
Another life,
That you just did not fit in.
Sometimes what is meant for you,
Is not straight forward.
Sometimes,
There are hurdles.
Sometimes,
There are hardships.
Sometimes,
There is heartbreak.
Sometimes,
There are disagreements.
Sometimes,
There are disappointments.
Sometimes,
Your path is not paved.
Sometimes,
Your path is bumpy.
Sometimes,
Your path will end.
Sometimes,
You will have to wait.
Wait and just be.
Just wait.
Until a new path shows up.
This path is yours,
All yours.
Settle for the wait.
Settle in,

Don't stop.
Don't stop believing.
Don't stop hoping.
Don't stop having faith.
Your time will come.
To settle,
For a life,
That just isn't yours.
Means to settle,
For less than you deserve.
Go all in.
All in,
To a life.
A life that is yours.
A life that feels good.
Until you find that,
Do not give up.
It won't be easy.
But what is for you,
Will find you.
It will find you.
That is for sure.
Never settle.
Be true to you.

This Shift

This shift I feel.
This shift in me.
This shift of reality.
Letting go of what I pictured.
Letting go of holding on.
Letting go of any outcome.
Moving into what might be.
Moving into the unknown.
Moving into unfamiliar.
Letting myself be.
Be uncomfortable.
Letting myself go.
Holding onto faith.
Trusting and surrender.
I will believe.
I will love.
I will be thankful.
I will have trust in myself.
I will ask for a sign.
I will wait until I must go.
I will wait.
I will be still.
Be still and know.
Be still and not know.
Be still and wait.
Be still then go.
Stillness is a gift.
I will cherish it.
This shift is stillness.
This shift is a rebirth.

This shift is a reprogram.
This shift is acceptance.
This shift is grief.
Grieving who I was.
And who I was supposed to be.
Grieving an illusion.
Grieving my old reality.
This shift.
This new me.
This shift in me.

We Are Who We Are

What do I need.
I don't know anymore.
I am changed.
I don't know where to start.
Loss has changed my heart.
Loss has changed my soul.
Loss has come over me.
I have to accept.
I have to let go.
I will never be the same.
Be the same again.
I won't be that same old me.
That same old me,
That everyone knows.
Loss tears you up inside.
It changes your heart.
It changes who you are.
My direction has changed.
So have my goals.
The way I look at the world,
Will never be the same.
The way I see people,
Is different now.
The way I go through life.
The way I understand.
The way I give my empathy.
I will take any judgement away.
I am not here to judge.
This no judgement zone.
I will try to understand.

Understand who you are.
Who you are,
And where you came from.
What you have experienced,
What you have endured.
We are who we are.
Because of what flows through us.
Because of what has happened.
Because of what we had to let go of.
Because of who enters our life.
Because of the events,
That we can't control.
The one thing I always thought I could control.
Was the way I loved.
The way I gave my love.
My heart loves.
My heart lets you in.
But what happens when,
You have to let go of what it holds?
Let go of that love.
This love that I have.
This love in my heart,
Has nowhere to go.
Loss of love has changed who I am.
Loss of love is loss of myself.
The love I held for you,
The love I held for me.
Letting go of love,
Means letting go of that part of myself.
The part of me who had love for you.
This is the process that is not expressed.
It is a process that cannot be explained.

This process may not be understood.
All of a sudden,
The person that you were.
That person,
Who loved.
That person,
Who lost.
That person is gone.
That person will grieve.
That grief is letting go.
Letting go of it all.
Letting go of that person,
That you once were.
Who am I now?
Where do I begin?
How do I explain this process?
Grief and loss will change who you are.
Grief and loss will change your life.
Let go.
Grieve.
What now?
Rebuild.
Reconstruct.
Bring on new beliefs.
Bring on this new self.
This new self you have made.

Little Bits

This feeling.
This feeling I hold.
This feeling within.
This feeling needs to flow through me.
But I won't allow it.
I won't allow it because of the pain.
The pain that I know, needs to be felt.
This pain is too strong.
This pain is too harsh.
This pain is so sharp.
This pain will take me over.
This pain will knock me over.
This pain will take my breath away.
It keeps coming up.
Coming up,
To be felt.
I am not ready.
I am not ready for it.
Deep breaths.
It's here.
It's here within me.
This pain.
These cries.
It's so overwhelming.
This feeling,
I know.
I know I need to feel it.
I know I have to welcome it.
I know I have to allow it.
This pain is love.

That I can no longer give.
The love I feel,
Is so beautiful.
How do I accept,
This loss I have?
How do I accept,
That you are not here to receive.
Receive this love,
I had in me.
This love for you,
I can't describe.
This love for you,
It hurts so much.
This love.
This pain.
This is mine to feel.
It is breaking my heart.
It is breaking my soul.
This love.
This pain.
It needs to flow.
Flow throughout me.
So that it can leave.
Breathe in.
Breathe out.
I can't even breathe.
This feeling in me.
It consumes each breath.
It consumes my heart.
Please allow it.
Please allow it.
It needs to be felt.

It needs to move through me.
I want it out.
The only way that it will leave,
Is if I face this pain.
The only way out,
Is through.
The only way out,
Is to hold it and love it.
Love my pain.
Love my grief.
Acknowledge it.
Feel it.
And then it will leave.
This pain.
It's strong.
Maybe it needs little bits at a time.
Let it come up,
Not all at once.
That's okay.
Whatever I need.
I know it is there.
I know it needs to move.
Just let it come up,
Little bits at a time.
Not all at once.
So that it consumes me.
Not all at once.
So that I can still breathe.
Just little bits.
Let little bits come.
Let little bits out.
Let little bits leave.

Today Is For Me

Up and down.
Around and around.
I don't know what I need.
I always know.
I know myself well.
But with this grief,
I don't.
This is new.
All new to me.
These moods that come.
They don't make sense.
These moods.
They aren't who I am.
I am all over the place.
I can't rationalize.
What I say,
Doesn't make sense.
These tears that come.
They come out of nowhere.
One minute I am angry.
The next minute,
I'm scared.
The very next minute,
I'm covered in tears.
My head hurts.
My body is a wreck.
I have aches that I have never had before.
I cry and cry.
I am moody and yell.
This anger comes with this sadness.

Why am I angry?
I wish it made sense.
But this is grief.
Grief will never make sense.
Grief is invisible.
Invisible to everyone.
Everyone, but me.
I look well,
To everyone else.
But my insides are a mess.
I can't even explain.
I just want to feel okay.
I am feeling these ups and downs.
I am the one,
Going around and around.
Please just feel this.
Get this out.
I must remind myself,
To have patience.
Have patience.
It's okay.
I am not put together.
Today is a very bad day.
Nothing makes sense.
Survival mode is on.
My attention span is gone.
I misplaced this,
And misplaced that.
I am just going through the motions.
All of these emotions are consuming me.
I am in these emotions.
And this is just how today is.

Today is here.
Today is for grief.
And that is just how it's going to be.
I won't try to change it.
I won't try to run from it.
I won't try to fix it.
I will just be in it.
Today is a bad day.
This is just how it is.
I designate today,
For me.
I designate today,
For my grief.
I designate today,
To feel my feelings.
This is today.
Today is for me.

I Will Decide

My voice.
My standards.
This love for myself.
I stick up for me.
I know what I need.
I will decide.
I will stand up for myself,
No matter what.
I respect who I am,
And the work that I've done.
This work.
These tears.
My whole self.
I will take care of me.
I will lift myself up.
I will speak my mind.
I will follow my gut.
I won't follow the crowd.
I will lead the way.
I am in control.
Control of my life.
I will decide.
Decide what's right.
What's right for me.
Where I must go.
Where I belong.
Where I end up,
It's up to me.
I will decide.
Decide for myself.

Give myself grace.
Surrender and trust.
Let go of the girl that I once was.
Let go of her hand.
Let go and have faith.
Have faith in my new self,
That I have made.
This girl.
This love.
I have this glow.
This glow in me,
That is shining bright.
This authenticity that I have found.
This new vibration.
My new calling.
This calling for me.
Is what is ahead.
This calling.
Is my future.
This calling.
Is my heart.
This calling.
This feeling.
This new start.

I Don't Need You Today

I am fighting my old self.
I am fighting hard.
I am fighting her.
She keeps coming back.
She keeps trying to drag me back.
Backwards.
She wants to go backwards.
She wants what she has left.
She wants what is not good for me.
I am fighting hard.
Her voice is loud.
She comes with my emotions.
She comes as my protector.
She craves what she knows.
She craves familiarity.
Emotional unavailability.
Emotional neglect.
She craves my old world.
She craves to be ignored.
She craves to help and nurture.
She wants to distract.
Find anything to distract.
What can she fix?
Who can she help?
This is my old self.
I am fighting her hard.
She comes as a protector.
She comes to protect.
Protect from these emotions.
These emotions that have come.

These emotions are here.
For me to feel.
She doesn't know to feel.
She was never taught.
She comes to protect.
Protect me from hurt.
She thinks she is in charge.
She thinks she holds the power.
I don't need you today.
I am trying to learn new ways.
I tell her this.
I am using my words.
Please back down.
I don't need you now.
Our life is different now.
Emotions are good.
Emotions need to be felt.
She honestly believes,
That hurting is bad.
She honestly believes,
To feel is not right.
She comes to fight these feelings.
Fight these feelings away.
She is pretty strong.
She is pretty loud.
I am fighting this urge.
This urge to allow.
Allow her to come through.
Allow her to protect.
I don't need you today.
I don't need you now.
Please take a step back,

And allow me to lead.
Feelings are good.
Pain is okay.
Facing our pain,
Will allow us to change.
Change and grow.
Become someone new.
I don't need you today.
I don't need you now.
Please take a step back.
I am here to feel.
If I feel this pain,
I can allow the joy in.
If I feel this grief,
I will also feel love.
This girl.
This protector.
She doesn't know love.
She doesn't even know.
She has no idea.
Please sit down.
Please step back.
I don't need this protection.
I've now got my own back.

New.

New.
New.
New.
Everything is new.
Everything is different.
Everything has changed.
Goodbye to the old.
The old.
Goodbye.
The old doesn't work.
Not anymore.
Create new ways.
Create new pathways.
Create new beliefs.
This new beginning.
New.
New.
New.
Bring on the new.
New is uncomfortable.
New is unfamiliar.
I am new.
I am refreshed.
This is my rebirth.
I am new.
The old is my past.
The old is there,
When I look back.
My old ways,
I don't need them anymore.

My old ways,
They no longer work.
My old ways,
No longer bring happiness.
Happiness to me.
Because the old is in my past.
I don't need my past.
Not anymore.
My past is behind me.
My past won't define me.
I have separated from my past.
I have come to terms with my past.
I have accepted my past.
My past is behind me.
I no longer need my past to haunt me.
Those old flashbacks.
Those old triggers.
I have worked through them.
I will put them behind me.
My past is old.
The old me.
My old self.
I had to grieve her.
Tell her goodbye.
The goodbye that took a pretty long time.
My goodbye to her,
Was extremely hard.
She kept me safe.
She kept me afloat.
She was so brave.
I send her love.
She is my idol.

She is in my past.
New.
New.
New.
It is time for new.
My new self.

These Old Stories

This girl is hurt.
She is really hurt.
She is angry.
She is sad.
She is looking for nurture.
These old stories.
Stories that she knows.
These old beliefs.
Beliefs that she knows.
These old stories.
These old beliefs.
They are not real.
It's time to let them go.
Let go of unworthiness.
Let go of abandonment.
Let go of rejection.
Let go of the anger.
It's time for forgiveness.
Forgive and let go.
Accept that these old stories,
Are not even real.
Let these stories come.
Let them come up.
Let them leave.
This manipulation,
Has really affected her.
This lack of protection,
Saddens her heart.
This lack of safety given to her,
Has made her have complete distrust.

Distrust in her people.
She doesn't trust what is said.
She doesn't trust your actions.
She doesn't trust because she has been left.
She doesn't trust because she has been burned.
She has been burned,
So many times.
She wants to trust.
She wants to have faith.
Have faith in the people that have stayed.
She has been so burned.
She has been so hurt.
This girl is hurt.
Nurture this girl.
Show her that trust can be believed.
Show her that trust is a new story.
Show her that people,
Can be believed in.
Guide her and acknowledge.
Acknowledge and hear her.
Hear her and see her.
She needs to feel heard.
She needs to feel seen.
This all needs to be acknowledged.
Before she can let go.
Let go of this story.
This story she knows.
This pain has been shoved down.
This pain has been dismissed.
This pain was too much,
For her to take in.
This pain was too much,

For her to feel.
She will feel this pain.
This pain from her past.
This old story, on repeat.
Creates more pain.
She will finally let it go.
Let go of this old story.
To create this new story.
This new story for her heart.
This new story of love.
She had this illusion.
This illusion of her life.
This illusion of love.
She accepted breadcrumbs.
Breadcrumbs of love,
Were given to her.
This was all that was given.
This was all that she knew.
She believed these breadcrumbs.
These breadcrumbs of love.
She was not shown true unconditional love.
She was not shown true trust.
She was not shown true safety and protection.
She was only given these breadcrumbs of love.
She has been betrayed.
By the ones who she trusted.
She has been betrayed.
By the ones she loved.
She was given lies.
She was given betrayal.
She was given abandonment.
She was given punishment.

She was given rejection.
She was given transactional love.
Love with conditions.
She was only loved,
When she became someone else.
She wore this mask,
In order to be loved.
This mask was not her,
She needed to take it off.
She found herself.
She found her soul.
She must be shown.
Shown in action.
Consistent action.
Genuine action.
Safety and protection.
It must be shown.
Words are words.
She won't believe them.
Words are easy to say.
She needs to see action.
Consistent action.
Consistent protection.
Consistency and authenticity.
These are qualities that she needs.
She needs you to stay,
And not run away.
She needs accountability,
And to stop being blamed.
Your actions are your actions,
They are not hers to take on.
Your problems are yours,

They are not hers to solve.
She needs you to stay when life gets hard.
She needs your effort,
Consistent effort.
She needs all of this to create her new story.
These old stories keep replaying.
They keep replaying.
Each time she is triggered.
Each time she feels left.
Each time she feels betrayed.
She knows she wants to let go of these old stories.
She knows these old stories.
They aren't even real.
She found her new circle.
Her new circle of love.
Her new circle creates new stories.
New stories she can trust.
She is on her way to believing these new stories.
She is working hard.
To let go of the old.
Let go of those old beliefs.
Let go of those old stories.
Let in the new.
Let in the love.

This Part Of Me

This part of me.
Needs to be loved.
This part of me,
Has only been half loved.
This part of me,
Has looked for external validation.
External validation.
External love.
This part has been trying to fill up.
Fill up externally.
Instead of facing the pain.
Facing this void.
This void within.
Grabbing for anything that easily distracts.
Distracts me from feeling.
Distracts me from seeing.
Seeing what's within.
Seeing what's inside.
It's easier to not see.
Not see the pain.
It's easier to have fun.
It's easier to laugh.
It's easier to crack jokes,
And make everyone laugh.
It's easier to feel good.
It's easier to live.
Live a life with only good.
Live a life shrugging everything off.
Live without pain.
Live without looking at my void.

It's easier to walk away.
Walk away from the discomfort.
It's easier to place the blame on everyone else.
It's easier to become who you really want to be.
It's easier to become her,
Without facing the pain.
Skipping over the hard parts.
Skipping to the end.
Skipping to your final goal.
Skipping ahead.
Skip the bad parts.
Skip the hard parts.
Just skip over.
Skip over it all.
Don't look.
Don't see.
Just cover it up.
There's no way you have a void.
This is the part.
The part of me.
I am ready to confront.
The part I am ready to see.
This is the part that has been hurting the most.
This is the part I've being avoiding for years.
This is the part I've been seeing in everyone else.
It is easier to see it in everyone else.
It is easier to just observe it.
Observe it when it's not you.
This is the part that has been in me.
She needs to be seen.
She needs to be heard.
She needs to cry these tears of hurt.

She needs to be held.
She needs to be fought for.
She needs to believe she is worth it.
I will tell this part,
You are worth it.
You are worthy.
You have always been good enough.
You should have been protected.
You should never have been dismissed.
I will teach you forgiveness.
No one is perfect.
You just needed me to validate these feelings.
These feelings you've had.
Had for so many years.
These feelings and blockages,
Keeping you from true love.
This has kept you from opening your heart.
Open your heart fully.
Keep it open with ease.
You'll never reach your soul.
If you don't remove this pain.
Remove these layers that have been covering it up.
Keeping you from your true self.
Your soul has been there all along.
This part of me.
Finally feels seen.
She finally feels heard.
I've listened to her.
I understand.
I understand her.
I'll ask her if she's ready.
Ready for me to hold her.

Hold her while she cries,
And feels this pain.
We'll sit in this void.
Together we'll sit.
This is real love.
This is what true love is.
This is unconditional.
I am showing you now.
I will never leave you,
I will only hear you.
Hear your call.
Hear your voice.
Hear your cries.
Hear your pain.
This is true love.
We had to learn it.
We had to find it.
We discovered this together.
On our journey.
Our journey to find unconditional love.
Our journey of letting go.
Letting go of what we know.
Taking the leap to discover our soul.
You were a part.
Just a part of me.
But together on this journey,
This part finally felt love.
Felt love from me.
Finally felt worthy.
Finally felt whole.

The Voice Of Fear

Discomfort is okay.
Discomfort is actually good.
Let yourself feel uncomfortable.
This discomfort is your sign.
Your sign of growth.
This discomfort is your leap.
The leap you were supposed to take.
Those regrets that creep in.
That is the voice of fear.
Your fear will speak, what is not real.
Just to get you to turn back around.
This fear will follow you.
Follow you down this path.
Filling you with thoughts.
Thoughts that are not even real.
Filling you with anything,
That leads you away from discomfort.
Your fear comes with discomfort.
Your fear wants you to stay.
Stay where you are.
Stay with what you know.
This fear, that comes.
Comes along.
Comes to bring you down.
Comes to throw you off.
Throw you off,
This heart driven path.
This fear that comes,
To keep you from love.
This emotion of fear.

It is opposite of love.
It will keep you from the light,
Your light inside.
This fear will keep you from consciousness.
Because it is in consciousness,
That you wake up.
It is consciousness,
That you see it all.
It is in consciousness,
That you find love.
To become conscious,
You must find your heart.
To become conscious,
You must understand.
Understand your emotions.
Understand your mind.
Understand the stories.
Understand what you are leaving behind.
Understand limiting beliefs.
Understand the process of letting go.
Understand your higher self,
Versus your ego.
Understand your voice of intuition.
Understand what comes from your soul.
Understand the voice of fear.
The voice of fear,
It is so loud.
You must learn to hear it.
Hear it and acknowledge it.
Once it feels acknowledged,
Then it will leave.
This voice of fear,

It comes to take over.
Take over your heart.
Take over your dreams.
Take over decisions.
Take over relationships.
Take over your gift.
Your gift you have found,
To give to the world.
This voice of fear.
It is only a voice.
This voice of fear.
It is not even real.
This voice of fear.
It will stand in the way.
Only if you allow it,
And let it stay.
It must be acknowledged.
Acknowledged with kindness.
"I don't need you today,
This is getting in my way."
Getting in the way,
Of finding your soul.
Getting in the way,
Of finding your truth.
This voice of fear,
Comes with discomfort.
Discomfort will come,
As you find your soul.
Discomfort will come,
Through all of the layers.
All of the layers,
That have been in the way.

This voice of fear,
Wants you to stay the same.
This voice of fear,
Wants to keep you from love.
Fear and love,
Don't get along.
But they come together.
It is a dance.
A dance of balance.
A dance of understanding.
Understanding that you are love.
You are not fear.
Fear just comes,
And then it will pass.
It is choosing love,
Every time.
But it is okay to feel the fear,
And then let it will leave.
Please don't fight it.
Just allow it.
Allow it to flow throughout your body.
Welcome it,
Then guide it.
Guide it through you.
It will flow through you,
And soon it will leave.
This voice of fear,
It will never stay.
Feelings are waves.
Waves that wash over you.
Waves that come.
Waves that leave.
This voice of fear,

It doesn't need an action.
This voice of fear,
Doesn't need a reaction.
This voice of fear,
Doesn't need a response.
All it needs,
Is to feel acknowledged.
To dismiss this fear,
Is to dismiss yourself.
To dismiss this fear,
Is to dismiss your voice.
To dismiss this fear,
Is to also dismiss love.
Let it in.
This fear will leave.
Trust this process.
This voice of fear,
It will become so quiet.
The more you trust yourself.
The more you love yourself.
The further along,
You get on this journey.
You are closer to love,
Than you ever have been.
This voice of fear,
It will come along.
This voice of fear,
Will come with love.
Have faith in love.
Trust in love.
The voice of fear,
It is meant to leave.

Take Care Of Me, Please

My feelings are mine.
They are mine.
I am responsible for me.
I am responsible for my feelings.
I look to myself.
I will keep myself safe.
I can't rely on anyone else.
There is a part of me,
That wants to be taken care of.
There is a part of me,
Who looks for my attachment figure.
This part of me,
Wants them to meet my needs.
Take care of me,
Please.
Meet my emotional needs.
Please be here.
And make decisions.
Take care of it all,
So, I don't have to.
There is no attachment figure,
To reach for.
They are out of sight.
It is only me.
I feel so weak,
While looking at this part.
This part of me,
Who felt so alone.
Who felt so unsafe.
Who felt so beat down.

This part of me,
She needs to be heard.
I will listen and hear her.
Give her what she needs.
As a little child,
No one was there.
They weren't there for her emotions.
They needed her.
She was there.
She put herself aside.
She sacrificed herself,
So many times.
Now she is here,
With these emotional needs.
She will learn to meet them.
She will have to feel.
I am here for her now.
I am holding her.
I tell her she's okay.
It's okay to be nervous.
It's okay to be a wreck.
It's okay to not be okay.
I am here for you to vent.
Vent it out.
I will hear you out.
Your emotions are important.
I will sit with you now.
We will do this together.
I will show you how.
I will show you how to feel.
I will hold space for you.
Hold space for your emotions.

Hold space for you to feel.
I will never neglect you.
I will never leave you.
Your emotional needs,
I will take care of.
I have changed my role.
I am not responsible,
For others.
I am responsible for me.
I am responsible for my feelings.
Take care of me,
Please.
I will say this to myself.
There is no attachment figure,
To reach out for.
My attachment figures.
It is not their job.
It is my job now.
I am learning how.
I am learning to take care of myself,
Now.
Take care of me,
Please.

This Weight

This debilitating feeling.
This debilitating wound.
This debilitating fight,
To feel this pain.
This weight you've been carrying.
All of this weight.
Sit here.
Sit in it.
It is time you face it.
It is time to heal.
This commitment.
Commitment to this wound.
Discovering the truth,
That has been inside of you.
Commitment to this weight.
Discovering this reality,
That was hidden from you.
Living in a world,
Hiding the truth.
Running from the pain.
Running from the truth.
Running from reality.
Running from the weight.
Creating an illusion.
Running from this pain.
Accepting the good,
And only the good.
Not seeing the bad.
Not seeing the hard.
Not seeing the truth.

All you knew was conditional love.
External validation.
Pretty words were love.
Manipulation and ego.
Rejection and punishment.
The responsibility put on you.
It was always your fault.
It was always you.
Refraining from using your own voice.
Pleasing everyone,
Except for yourself.
Going through the motions,
Pushing it all down.
Suppress all of your feelings.
Push it all away.
Sabotage yourself.
Sacrifice yourself.
Abandon yourself,
For everyone else.
It is easier this way,
Was what you were told.
Shrug it off.
It's not a big deal.
Keep moving forward,
While suppressing the pain.
You don't need to have feelings.
You are too emotional.
Overly sensitive.
The emotional one.
Afraid to be judged.
Afraid to be seen.
Be seen for who you are.

Who you really are.
Because who you really are,
Was never really accepted.
You didn't feel safe.
Your feelings were minimized.
They were dismissed.
No one sat with you,
While you cried.
People ran away,
When you needed them the most.
So, you learned to be here,
For yourself.
Honor yourself now.
Honor these feelings.
These feelings that weren't heard.
These feelings were dismissed.
It is time for you now.
Take care of yourself now.
All of your needs.
All of your feelings.
You have needs.
You will meet them.
You will hear them.
You will honor them.
This is your responsibility.
This healing is yours.
It is all yours.
The responsibility is on you now.
You have shifted the blame.
No one is to blame.
Not anymore.
This took a long time,

For you to see.
This took a long time,
For you to reach.
Reach this point,
Of forgiveness.
You understand forgiveness.
This forgiveness is here.
Acceptance and forgiveness.
These come together.
Once you accept,
This weight is lifted.
The weight you've been carrying,
All along.
All this time.
This weight is gone.

Ready

You have to be ready.
Ready to see.
See the truth.
See reality.
See the illusion.
You have to be ready.
Ready to uncover.
Uncover your wounds.
You must be ready.
To go into your wounds.
Your wounds are not pretty.
Your wounds are unsettling.
Your wounds are messy.
They are chaotic.
You must be willing,
To sit in the pain.
You must be willing,
To leave your old identity.
Sit in your wounds.
Sit in these feelings.
Sit in the uncomfortable.
Sit in the unfamiliar.
You must be willing,
To make this commitment.
This commitment to healing.
Healing for yourself.
This healing is solitude.
This healing is understanding.
Understanding everything you knew,
It is not what is real.

Stop projecting what you want to see.
Stop projecting your old reality.
Your old reality onto what is here now.
You are seeing through your own lens.
Your lens of trauma.
Your lens of limiting beliefs.
Your lens of the past.
Your lens of what you've been through.
Wash this lens off.
Are you ready to see?
See what is real.
See through the illusion.
See past your wounds.
The only way through,
Is to feel.
You can't bypass.
These unhealed wounds,
Will come out somehow.
They will make their way through.
They will leak into,
These new relationships that you have built.
These unhealed wounds.
They will make an appearance.
Unless you heal them.
Heal these wounds.
Heal them now.
Just sit here now.
Sit in this wound.
It will be worth it.
I promise it will.
Sit here now.
Be here now.

This will all be worth it.
Someday you will see.
For now,
Just admit.
Admit that you are ready.
Ready to feel.

This Role

I took you out of your role.
The role that you have been in,
Your whole life.
The role that made you feel worthy.
This role that you played so well.
I took you away from all that you knew.
I took you away from all of your people.
I will show you a new place.
A new place for you.
A new place where you don't need a role.
This new place.
Allows you to be.
Be who you are.
Who you truly are inside.
I know you feel completely out of place.
I know you feel like your identity is gone.
I know you have left your comfort zone.
Your role you knew.
Is no longer there.
You are not the fixer.
You are not the lifter.
You don't know what,
To do with yourself.
Now that this codependency is gone.
I took you away.
Away from that world.
That world where you,
Found worth in your role.
You are not your role.
You are not here to fix.

You are not here to be there for everyone else.
You are not here to please.
You are not here to serve.
You are not here to sacrifice yourself anymore.
I know this is,
So hard to see.
I know this is,
So hard to understand.
The girl you thought you were,
Is no longer there.
I am showing you new.
I am showing you how to heal.
Heal from this role,
That you thought was yours.
This role won't be played by you anymore.
I am giving you permission,
To leave this role.
Your friendships where you played this role.
They must come to an end.
You are not this girl.
You have changed.
Your mask is off.
This façade that you have put on,
No longer works.
This façade was there,
For your protection.
For your protection,
Because you didn't feel safe.
Your friendships.
Your people.
Your relationships.
All of these must start over.

Begin again.
Begin with the girl you are now.
This girl,
You truly are.
This is you.
You are free.
Free from this role.
This role that you've played.
You must allow yourself to grieve.
Go through these emotions.
Feel them and let go.
You now understand,
Why you had to go.
Why you had to leave,
People you loved.
People who loved you,
In this role.
You have found your soul.
You have found trust in me.
I am showing you the way.
Please have faith in me.
I promise I won't guide you wrong.
I am listening to our intuition.
It is so strong.
I am listening to our gut.
I am connected to our soul.
Because of this,
It is okay to leave your role.
This role was not you.
It never was.
This role you played.
Helped everyone else,

Be who they are.
You were there,
For everyone else.
This role.
This girl.
You did it for everyone else.
You never did it for you.
And now it is time.
It is time for YOU.
Time for YOU now.
You are done playing a role.
You are now loved for you.

This Cage

She is making progress,
In her new world.
She is loving herself.
She is giving herself nurture.
She is giving herself love.
She is meeting her needs.
She is there for her comfort.
She is there for safety and protection.
She is using her voice.
She is learning this.
She is making progress,
In her new world.
She is finding her worth.
She is finding her love.
She is giving herself what she always needed.
She always looked to the outside world.
She always looked for external love.
She always looked for validation from others.
She didn't believe in herself at all.
Codependency was what she knew.
She had to break out of this cage.
This cage she was in.
This cage was all she knew.
This cage was preventing her,
From being herself.
This cage kept her hostage.
This cage controlled her.
This cage fooled her.
This cage of manipulation.
This was what she knew.

"Manipulate me please."
This is what went on.
Went on in this cage.
This cage she was in.
She was in for so long.
Her whole life,
Inside of this cage.
This cage,
Where she didn't have love for herself.
"This is what I am worthy of."
"This is what I deserve."
"This is all I know."
"This is familiar to me."
"This is my comfort zone."
"Talk to me, anyway you please."
This is what went on.
Inside of this cage.
This cage she was in.
Until she broke free.
She found love for herself.
She found herself worthy.
Worthy of it all.
Worthy of love.
Love for herself.
She deserved it all.
She deserved the best.
As soon as she believed this.
She kicked open the door.
This door of this cage.
This cage she was in.
She will never go back.
This cage is done.

This cage is destroyed.
She will never go back.
She will no longer accept.
Accept manipulation.
Accept manipulation as love.
She taught herself this.
She freed herself.
She will no longer be talked down to.
She will no longer be dismissed.
She will no longer be ignored.
She will no longer be left.
She will no longer,
Allow her worth to be shattered.
She will no longer,
Allow others to destroy her.
Because she knows her worth.
She knows what it took,
To get herself out.
Out of this cage.
This was not easy.
She said what was real.
She called it out every time.
No one in this cage,
Appreciated this.
This was not allowed here.
She would be dismissed.
Her words were dismissed.
Her voice was shut down.
She was given punishments.
She was given the silent treatment.
She was rejected.
She was betrayed.

She was left.
She was not considered.
These are the rules inside of this cage.
This cage she was in.
This cage that she lived in.
These rules,
Were not accepted.
Accepted by her.
She will put up a fight.
She will rebel against these rules.
These rules of this cage.
This cage that she was in.
She will not obey these rules.
These rules of this cage.
She will not behave,
The way others want her to behave.
She will be herself.
She will honor herself.
She always did,
She always will.
She accepted the punishment,
That was given to her.
"This is just how it is."
Until the day.
She stopped.
She stopped accepting punishments,
And rejection.
She stopped accepting treatment,
She never deserved.
She stopped pleasing these people.
She stopped putting herself aside.
She stopped trying to fix,

What was never hers to fix.
She stopped putting her energy,
Into anything but herself.
She thought this was the way of the world.
She thought this was how it was supposed to be.
She thought this was normal.
This cage she was in.
This cage was a world,
She never belonged in.
This cage was never hers.
This cage held her prisoner,
Along with her beliefs.
She broke free.
She picked up her worth.
She picked up her faith.
She picked up her voice,
Along the way.
On her way out,
She grabbed these tools.
These tools she would need.
To break free of this cage.
These are the tools,
That she will carry with her.
Carry with her,
In this new world.
She is free now.
Free of this cage.
She is free now.
She has her own little world.

Her Gifts

She has this anger.
This anger in her.
This anger she will feel.
This anger will be released.
She is angry.
Angry that she was not treated,
The way she should have been.
She has this huge heart.
She shares it with the world.
She shared it with people.
People who destroyed her.
People who have hurt her.
She sees the good.
The good in everyone.
She learns who people are,
So that she can understand.
Understand why they are,
The way that they are.
She learns who people are.
She learns their pain.
She learns their past history,
So that she can understand.
She will always find compassion.
Compassion for their pain.
She will always find compassion.
Even when she is treated poorly.
She understands why,
People are the way they are.
She will always look past this poor behavior.
Because deep down.

Deep down in her soul.
This was always what she wanted to be given.
She wanted to be understood.
She wanted to be learned.
She wanted to be heard.
She wanted to be seen.
She was in pain,
So, she acted out.
She just wanted to be figured out.
She didn't understand,
Why people didn't put the effort.
The effort in,
To understand her.
So, this will be her gift.
Her gift to the world.
Her gift of understanding.
Her gift of compassion.
She will learn who you are.
She will understand,
Why you are the way you are.
She will understand,
Where these rebellious acts come from.
She will understand,
Why you shut people out.
She will understand,
Why you push people away.
She will understand,
When you are filled with shame.
She has learned you.
So, she understands.
And all that she asks,
Is for you to not hurt her.

Hurt people,
Hurt people.
This is her lesson.
This lesson she has learned.
She has learned it over and over.
She has learned it a thousand times.
She finally learned this lesson.
She understands all of these times,
That she has been hurt.
It has nothing to do with her.
It is the pain inside of you.
She understands this now.
She will understand.
But she will protect herself better,
Than she ever has before.
This anger she has.
This anger in her.
This anger is from all of the times,
She has been burned.
She has been burned.
She has been so deeply hurt.
She has been betrayed so many times.
She has been walked on.
She has been talked down to.
She has been dismissed.
She has not been considered.
Her voice has been shut down.
Her boundaries weren't respected.
Almost like she didn't matter.
Like she was unimportant.
She will take her power back now.
By understanding, that all of these actions.

All of these actions came from pain.
Pain inside of people she loved.
Pain that they did not want to see.
Pain that they would put on her,
So, they didn't have to face their darkness within.
She understands this now.
This will help her anger.
Other people's actions,
Have nothing to do with her.
She understands this now.
Other people's choices.
Those choices are theirs.
Those choices,
Have nothing to do with her.
Her gift of understanding.
Her gift of compassion.
Her gift of empathy,
Will now stand protected.
She will protect these gifts.
She will keep these gifts to herself.
And she will give them out,
When she feels safe.
She will give them out,
When you treat her with love.
When you treat her the way she deserves.
She will learn to trust.
Have trust in you.
Trust that you don't treat her,
The way she's been treated in the past.
Trust won't come quickly for her.
Trust will be earned.
Because of how many times,

She has been burned.
Her heart.
Her love.
Her gifts.
Her empathy.
Her understanding.
Her compassion.
These all are her gifts.
These gifts that she has to give.
She has learned to keep them safe.
Her gift to the world,
Will just have to be earned.
She will observe.
Her body will tell her.
Her intuition will always guide her.

These Storms

I heard my soul call.
Through the storms.
The storm within me.
These thunderstorms.
So much rain.
So much wind.
So much darkness.
So many storms.
Never ending.
Continuous.
These storms.
On repeat.
Over and over.
Blackness.
It's dark.
Dark again.
Sitting in these storms.
All alone.
Fighting by myself.
Listening to the rain.
Watching the lightning.
The storm clouds roll in.
Finding shelter.
To sit once again.
Once again,
In another storm.
Another one comes.
I am sitting with faith.
Right next to me.
Each time a storm comes,

It brings more and more light.
These storms brighten,
Just the smallest bit.
This light is my soul.
Uncover it.
Let these storms come.
Let them pass.
I am not scared.
Not anymore.
I know why they are here,
To bring me my light.
This light.
Glimmers.
Glimmers and shines.
This light is bright.
I see through the storms.
It used to be,
That when storms would come.
I couldn't see light.
Light through the storms.
There would never be light.
Light in the dark.
But that has changed.
That has changed now.
These storms,
Aren't as bad.
These storms,
Aren't as long.
These storms.
They come.
And then they pass.
There is more and more light.

Through each storm.
These storms in me.
These storms within me.
These thunderstorms.
They are here,
To show me my light.
I see my light.
I grab for it.
I know I deserve it,
Because I have fought for it.
My light is here.
My light is my soul.
I heard it calling,
Through all of these storms.
This light is mine.
I finally have it.
This light within me,
Has replaced these storms.

New Beliefs

These limiting beliefs.
They come to the surface.
They rise within me,
So that I can hear.
I can hear what has been inside.
Been inside me all along.
They come to the surface,
So that they can be released.
These limiting beliefs.
These beliefs in me.
These old beliefs are not helpful anymore.
They never were.
But that,
I didn't know.
I didn't know what was holding me back.
Holding me back,
All of this time.
All of this time,
Driven by my subconscious.
All of this time,
These limiting beliefs held me back.
I had no idea.
These were inside.
I had no idea.
This is what my inner girl has been hearing.
She has been hearing these thoughts,
This whole time.
These limiting beliefs,
They don't serve me anymore.
These limiting beliefs,

I don't need them anymore.
I never did.
But I didn't know.
I wasn't aware,
Of what was within.
It is hard to see.
It is hard to look at.
It is hard to understand,
That these were my beliefs.
Let them go.
It is time.
I am worthy.
I am good enough.
I will free myself from these chains.
These chains of beliefs.
Beliefs that were not real.
Beliefs that I never should have known.
I decide now.
I decide what I hear.
I will form new beliefs.
Beliefs in me.
I will start with,
I am worthy.
I am worthy of it all.
I deserve it all.
Let these other thoughts go.
Let them free.
Let them out.
Out of me.
Time for release.
A huge release.
These limiting beliefs,

They are not real.
Please don't believe them.
This is not me.
This is another layer,
That has come through.
This layer in me,
It is at the surface.
This layer has come,
To be released.
This layer.
It is here.
I am hearing it now.
This has been blocking me,
From what I need.
Replace these beliefs.
Beliefs that serve me.
Beliefs that stand for,
All that I am.
I am me.
I will form new beliefs.
These new beliefs in me,
Will set me free.
Free from these chains.
These chains of limiting beliefs.
I will start over,
With new beliefs.
Beliefs that signify all that I am.

My Subconscious

Driven by,
What is in my subconscious.
My subconscious holds my wounds.
My subconscious knows what I have been through.
I am driven by,
What is inside.
Inside of my subconscious.
Beliefs that I hold.
Hold of myself.
Beliefs that I hold.
Hold of the world.
Beliefs that I hold.
Stories that were told.
Stories that I heard.
Stories that I observed.
All of this,
Is held in my subconscious.
I kept it there.
I lived on the surface.
I lived without knowing my shadow.
My shadow side.
Living on the surface.
It was nice.
Living on the surface.
It was easy.
Living on the surface.
I had no self-awareness.
I was not aware,
Of what was inside.
Deep inside.

Deep within.
I finally made time,
To go inside.
Time to go inward.
Time to face my wounds.
Now I understand,
That my behavior was being driven.
Driven by this pain.
This pain within me.
I was being driven,
By subconscious beliefs.
I will change this.
I will stay on this path.
I commit myself.
I commit to an unravel.
I will travel down this path.
This path into my subconscious.
My subconscious wounds.
New behaviors.
New habits.
New stories and beliefs.
I get to choose.
I get to decide.
I am seeing so clear.
I finally understand.
This path of healing.
Healing my subconscious.

What Is Best For You

Stand up for yourself.
This is what you have learned.
You will stand up for yourself,
No matter what.
It doesn't matter what they say.
It doesn't matter how they respond.
It doesn't matter if they leave.
All that matters,
Is that you use your voice.
Use your voice.
Stand up for yourself.
You are worthy.
You deserve to be treated well.
You will not put up with anything,
But.
Anything but,
Being treated well.
You have put up with so much.
You have let a lot slide.
You have let so much go.
Your voice has been shut down.
What you have to say,
Has been dismissed.
You have been yelled at.
You have been gas lit.
You have been manipulated.
You have been left.
You have stood up for yourself,
More and more.
You bring up what is wrong.

You speak the truth.
You are learning to do,
What is best for you.
You come out with your feelings.
You call them out.
This may not be,
What they want to hear.
But that is okay,
That is on them.
It is not your problem,
When they react.
They can have a reaction.
They can make a choice.
Whatever they choose,
It is not on you.
It is not on you,
To carry that burden.
It is not on you,
To make them stay.
It is not on you,
To fix it all.
You will do,
What is best for you.
Sometimes people come,
Just for a short time.
Sometimes people come,
To give you a lesson.
Sometimes people won't like what you say.
Sometimes people can decide,
They want to go a different way.
Just like you.
Just like you can decide.

You hold the power.
You make the choice.
You can decide if they are good for you.
You can walk away,
Whenever you want.
You don't have to put up with,
Poor treatment.
You don't have to put up with,
Being dismissed.
You don't have to put up with,
One sided friendships.
You don't have to put up with,
Being treated like an object.
You will do,
What is best for you.
You can walk away,
At any time.
This is your life.
You get to choose.
You get to put up with,
Whatever is good for you.

She Took The Strength

I now understand,
How my past has affected me.
I now understand,
These wounds I have.
I understand completely.
I see it all so clear.
My old self,
She didn't have a voice.
She didn't speak up,
Out of fear.
She didn't speak up,
Because she didn't feel safe.
She didn't say a word,
Because she didn't have strength.
She appeared controlling.
She appeared dominant.
Controlling because her world was falling apart.
She wanted to control,
Any little thing.
Any little thing she could control.
Her world was chaos.
And she kept adding more and more burdens,
To carry.
She was reactive.
She didn't have boundaries.
She didn't know how to use her voice.
She didn't know how to create a safe space.
She was torn down.
Her heart was shattered.
She didn't know how to live like this.

She became someone else.
Someone she wasn't.
She created a character.
She created this character,
For everyone else.
She couldn't be herself,
Because she didn't feel safe.
She did this for love.
She did this for protection.
She did this because she wasn't shown.
She wasn't shown to be herself.
She wasn't really accepted when she was herself.
She felt shut down anytime she tried.
She was ignored.
She was betrayed.
She was lied to.
She was left.
She was scolded.
She was punished.
She was surrounded by people.
People who didn't understand her.
They didn't understand.
They didn't put in the effort.
Put in the effort to piece all of this together.
Why was she this way?
Why was she pulling away?
Why was she running away?
Why was she acting out?
She needed to be observed.
She needed to be understood.
She needed to just be herself.
She needed to just be.

Let her just be.
Her behavior didn't need to be taken personally.
Her behavior was always made to be about them.
There was a reason for her behavior.
This reason was pain.
This reason was hurt.
This reason was devastation.
This reason was anger.
This reason was sadness.
There were so many reasons for her behavior.
She was told she was bad,
So many times.
Her voice was shut down and dismissed,
Multiple times.
Her mother left her,
When she needed her the most.
Her father didn't hear her,
When she spoke.
Her parents didn't protect her.
Her parents left her.
They neglected her,
For their own needs.
They neglected her,
For themselves.
They put themselves,
First.
And she came last.
She always came last.
She felt like she had to compete.
Compete for love,
And always be good.
Always be agreeable.

Never speak up.
Walk on eggshells.
Say what they want to hear,
And don't disagree.
Love was taken.
Taken away.
If she did something,
That was against what they said.
They threatened her.
They punished her.
They also left her.
This was the way,
It always was.
It was their way,
Or no way.
It was the right way.
Or the wrong way.
This black and white world,
With very little grey.
She had to get out.
Out of this world.
She wanted to repair.
Repair these wounds.
Repair this pain.
This pain in her.
Her childhood wounds were created.
They were created,
And she kept living.
She didn't acknowledge.
Acknowledge this pain.
Acknowledge these wounds.
She just wanted to escape.

Escape the pain.
She wanted to run.
Run from the pain.
She wanted to run.
Run from her wounds.
Until she stopped.
Until she realized it was finally time.
Finally time,
To feel her pain.
She left her old world,
And there was finally room.
Room to feel.
Room to heal.
She made room.
She made space.
She finally found safety.
She finally stopped running.
Running from herself.
Running from what was within.
Running from what she was hiding.
Her authentic self was buried underneath it all.
This is where I come in.
I am here because of her.
Because she took the strength,
To uncover her wounds.
She took the strength,
To feel her pain.
She took the strength,
To follow her heart.
She took the strength,
And found her soul.
Uncover me.

She did this for me.
She did this to find our authenticity.
And this is what makes it so hard,
To say goodbye.
Goodbye to her.
To my old self.

Reparent

What is a father?
And what does this look like?
What is a mother?
And what does this look like?
I wish I had a father to look up to.
I wish I had a father to protect me.
My father failed to keep me safe.
My father failed to protect me.
My father failed because he couldn't see.
He couldn't see reality.
He had a false perception,
Of reality.
He had an illusion of life.
He couldn't see properly.
He never took the time,
To figure himself out.
He never took the time,
To love himself.
He never took the time,
To lift his worth.
He never took the time,
To make himself healthy.
He never took the time,
To become a man.
Same with my mother.
My mother never took the time.
Took the time to love herself.
She never took the time to figure out who she is.
She never took the time to find her identity.
She relied on a husband.

She relied on someone to take care of her.
Someone who brought her down.
Someone who wasn't good for her.
He didn't allow her to be herself.
He was controlling,
And ruined her.
He shut her down,
And made her into what he wanted her to be.
These were my parents.
This is what I knew.
It is time to release.
Release what I know.
Release the pain.
Release my past.
This is my job.
My job now.
To reparent myself.
Give myself the mother I never had.
Give myself the father I never had.
It is now time.
It is up to me.
No more playing the victim.
I am taking responsibility.
Responsibility for my life.
My life is up to me.
It is my turn.
I will choose.
I will protect.
I will give myself,
The love I never had.
The love I didn't receive,
I will give it to myself.

It is up to me now.
It is time.
Time to reparent.
Reparent myself.
I am in control.
Control of my life.

The Final Outcome

There is no rush.
To an outcome.
To the final outcome.
There is no rush.
It is not a race.
A race to the end.
A race to the finish line.
There is no hurry.
Hurry to the conclusion.
The conclusion to her story.
There is no rush to make a decision.
The final decision.
There is no rush.
There is no hurry.
She will take her time.
She will know,
When it is time.
The final outcome.
The finish line.
The conclusion.
The final decision.
There is no plan.
There is no plan,
That needs to be made.
Life doesn't always go as planned.
Life has a way,
Of just going with the flow.
Finding what is in alignment,
With her soul.
That takes time.

There is no rush.
Just be still.
Be still and know.
Know and trust,
That the final outcome will just end up.
End up being whatever it is.
Whatever is supposed to be.
It will just be.
Trust and surrender.
Wait with patience.
Release and let go.
The answer will come.
It may come as a faint whisper.
It may come as a sign.
It may come disguised as a person.
A person who brings a message.
A message to you.
It may come as an opportunity.
An opportunity for you.
It may come with disruption and chaos.
It may come as a sensation in your body.
It may come as a click in your brain.
It may come as a moment.
A moment of clarity.
Clarity of the answer.
The answer to the final outcome.

Bravery

What is bravery?
Bravery takes courage.
Bravery is going beyond.
Beyond your line.
Bravery is going beyond what you think.
What you think you can do.
Bravery is going beyond the point.
Beyond the point that takes you down.
Bravery is moving straight into fear.
Straight into fear without looking back.
Bravery is walking side by side.
Side by side with each emotion.
Each emotion you don't want to feel.
Bravery is letting yourself feel.
Feeling every emotion.
Every emotion that comes.
Bravery is vulnerability.
Bravery is facing your tears,
Letting them flow down your face.
Bravery is allowing yourself to be seen.
Bravery is opening your heart.
Open your heart to the world.
Bravery is spreading love.
Spreading love everywhere you go.
Bravery is having the audacity.
The audacity of walking into the unknown.
Bravery is sharing.
Sharing your soul.
Bravery is persistence.
Persistence in trusting.

Trusting in yourself.
Bravery is taking the chance.
Taking the chance to fail.
Taking a risk.
A risk that might fail.
Bravery is getting back up.
And trying again.
Bravery is putting perfection down.
Bravery is letting go of control.
Bravery is trusting in what is.
Bravery is an act of strength.
An act of strength of what is inside.
Inside of you.
Bravery is looking within.
Looking at yourself is extremely brave.
Bravery is about being different.
Standing out from the crowd.
Bravery is about not belonging.
Not belonging to anyone but yourself.
Bravery is standing tall.
Even when you feel so small.
Bravery is admitting your flaws.
Bravery is about showing your weakness.
Bravery is an act of courage.
Bravery is confrontation.
Confronting reality.
Confronting the illusion.
Bravery is speaking the truth.
Bravery is using your voice.
Bravery is staying.
Staying when it gets hard.
Bravery is also walking away.

Walking away if it's right for you.
Bravery is fighting.
Fighting for love.
Fighting for yourself.
Bravery is making decisions.
Decisions that benefit you,
And not other people.
Bravery is deciding to be authentic.
Bravery is genuine.
Bravery is courageous.

This Is Reality

I know that your mood today,
Is not what you want it to be.
I know that you really want to be happy,
And carefree.
I know that you really want to be enjoying life.
I know that you want a smile on your face.
I know that you want to dance,
Like nothing matters.
Dance in the rain,
Like that's all life is.
I know that you really just want to pretend.
Pretend like you are not hurting.
Pretend like your past didn't happen,
But it did.
I know that you want to run away.
Run away from your problems,
Like you always have.
Run away from the pain.
Run away from this day.
Run away from feeling this way.
I know that you really want to laugh.
Laugh without pain.
Laugh without hurt.
Laugh without betrayal.
Laugh it all off.
Laugh it off.
Dance it off.
Shrug it off.
Run it off.
Beach it off.

Just run away from it all.
I know you really want all the good things.
I know you really wish life was different.
I know you really don't want to feel any of this.
I know you feel like you are the only one.
I know you feel like you are missing out.
Missing out on a life.
A life that should be yours.
A life that you will make.
Make for yourself.
A life that isn't lived for everyone else.
This is reality.
Bad things have happened.
You have to digest it all.
This is now.
It's okay to be down.
It's okay to frown.
It's okay to rest.
It's okay to just be.
It's okay to not be happy.
Be happy all the time.
It's okay to admit.
Admit to healing.
Healing for yourself.

Where The Wildflowers Are

In the grass.
Where the wildflowers are.
Laying in the grass,
With the sun,
Up above.
The warmth of the sun,
On my skin.
I soak up the sun.
I soak it all in.
Nature is calling.
Calling me.
Nature is where I ground myself.
Grounding myself into the earth.
My feet in the grass.
Where the wildflowers are.
The smell of the flowers.
The sound of the birds.
The branches above me.
The wind blows the leaves.
I am laying here on the ground.
This is right where I belong.
Right where the wildflowers are.

Please Don't

Please don't fix me.
I am not your charity case.
I am me,
Embracing my flaws.
Please don't try to fix who I am.
I am just coming out to be real.
Please don't try to change what I am feeling.
I am feeling this,
And that is just what it is.
Please don't try to cheer me up.
It is not your job,
To cheer me up.
Please don't try to change my world.
This is my world,
Right now.
This is it.
Please don't try to fix my problem,
I am here just trying to accept what is.
Please don't try to make it better.
Right now in this moment,
I need to be here.
I need to be in this.
This is my path.
I don't need you to try to change my path.
If I need something,
I will ask.
If I need you to do something,
I will say it.
I don't need you guessing what I need.
I don't need you offering your help.

All I need is to be understood.
All I need is to be heard.
I don't need you to assume anything.
I would say words,
If they needed to be said.
I don't need you to step in.
All I need is for you to listen.
Listen to my words.
I know what I need.
I am not going to beat around the bush.
I will speak the truth.
I will use my voice.
I appreciate you wanting to help,
Oh, so much.
I appreciate you trying to fix.
I appreciate your efforts.
Believe me,
I do.
I appreciate you being here,
I really can't thank you enough.
It is just getting old.
When my words aren't heard.
While I am here,
And I keep being misunderstood.
I am seen for someone I am not.
I am seen through your lens.
I am seen through the trauma that you've been
through.
I am not being seen.
Seen for me.
Seen for who I am.
Seen for what's inside.

You just assume you know,
But you don't ask.
You don't ask because of what is inside of you.
You just want to think you know.
Think you know me.
Think you know what I need.
You think this is the right thing.
You think I need what you need.
But I am not you.
I am me.

I See Myself

I see myself.
I see myself clear now.
My old self.
I could not see.
My old self,
Did not have self-awareness.
My old self,
Saw through a lens.
A lens of my unprocessed trauma.
Unprocessed emotions that I shoved down.
I saw through a lens.
A lens of pain.
A lens I built throughout my childhood.
Throughout my life.
I did not want to see myself.
I didn't know how.
All I knew.
Was this lens.
I didn't know,
How to process my trauma.
I didn't know,
How to process my pain.
My pain I took on.
My pain I experienced.
I did not want to look.
I did not want to see.
I did not want to face reality.
What it did to me,
The impact of this pain.
The impact of heartbreak.

The impact.
The toll it took on me.
I just formed walls.
Walls that kept me safe.
Walls that kept me from my own self.
Walls that kept me from vulnerability.
Walls that kept me from processing my pain.
Walls that kept me.
Kept me from reality.
These walls prevented me.
From seeing clear.
These walls prevented me,
From my own growth.
These walls prevented me.
Prevented me from love.
Love and connection.
Acceptance and compassion.
The walls became an illusion.
This illusion,
Was all I could see.
I couldn't see the love.
The love that surrounded me.
I also couldn't see the pain.
My pain inside of me.
I couldn't feel the pain.
I also could not feel love.
The love that was given to me.
I could not feel anything,
I was just numb.
Anytime I showed myself,
And I felt shutdown.
Anytime I became myself,

And I was put down.
Anytime I spoke up,
And was not heard.
Another layer I built.
I kept adding and adding.
Adding these walls.
Walls that could not be seen.
Seen by anyone, not even me.
My people around me thought this was me.
But this was not me at all.
This was me,
Covered in walls.
This was me,
With layers of protection.
This was me.
A me that I built.
A me that I made.
A me that did not feel at all.
A me that was numb.
This unemotional me.
This me,
Was who everyone loved.
But this was not me at all.
I became someone else.
Someone that wasn't me.
Someone who was made up of walls.
Someone who kept her emotions to herself.
Someone who did not speak up.
Someone who chose not to feel.
Not feel at all.
Someone who was not available.
Available,

Emotionally at all.
And when I decided to take down my walls.
When I decided to process my pain,
My whole world needed to change.
Change, drastically.
A sudden change.
I had different needs.
I spoke differently.
I used my voice,
That no one ever heard.
No one ever heard this me before.
This was a side,
That no one ever saw.
Little did they know,
This was the real me.
I started feeling my feelings.
I started sharing my feelings.
I started facing my pain.
I started to become real.
I was honest with myself,
Finally.
A lot of the people around me,
Did not like this new girl.
This new girl, emerging.
This new girl was me.
The real me,
That they really didn't know.
A lot of them would leave.
A lot of them would not stay.
Removing these layers,
Piece by piece.
Each wall I took down.

Each layer I faced,
Was unprocessed pain.
Pain, I shoved down,
So that I didn't have to feel.
I didn't have to look at.
I didn't have to see.
I started to understand.
Understand this illusion.
My illusion I made,
To protect myself.
This illusion kept me safe.
It was part of my walls.
These walls,
That no one could see.
Not even me.
I really believed this was who I was.
Until I realized.
I could not feel.
I could not feel at all.
I was numb.
Numb inside.
I needed to stop fixing and helping others,
And heal myself.
Fixing was my defense.
My defense mechanism.
To look at everyone else.
Look at them,
Not myself.
I let go of this.
This was not my job.
This was not my responsibility.
My job is me.

I need to look at myself.
To heal myself,
I will take down these walls.
I will start to have trust.
Have trust in the world.
Have trust in myself.
Have trust in my voice.
I will leave behind,
Everything I know.
My defense mechanisms.
How I cope.
Everything must change.
Everything must go.
I am attached to nothing.
I will love myself.
I will love myself more,
Than I ever did before.
I will show myself.
I will become this person.
This girl,
Who I was meant to be.
Always meant to be,
But was covered in pain.
Covered by walls.
Walls that I don't need.
Not anymore.
I will be myself now.
Myself without walls.
I will be this girl now.

Unsafe

To feel unsafe.
This was what I needed to face.
I felt so unsafe.
Unsafe in the world.
Unsafe around everyone.
So, I built an escape.
I built these walls.
Walls around my heart.
Walls around my soul.
I felt so unsafe.
Unsafe in my own life.
I didn't feel safe,
And I didn't even know.
I couldn't feel pain.
I couldn't feel love.
I shut myself off.
All of my emotions were off.
I was running from myself.
I was running away.
All I could do was numb.
Numb myself from the pain.
Numbing became my way.
I didn't want to face anything.
I didn't want to see.
I didn't want to hear.
I wasn't ready.
Distractions and running.
Fill my life up.
Fill my life with plans,
Don't ever stop.

Keep going and going.
Help everyone else.
I'm good at that,
Not looking at myself.
Don't look inside.
Keep everyone out.
I've been burned and betrayed,
That is what I know.
Keep myself safe.
Keep these walls up.
All while I am doing this,
I won't let love in.
I won't feel love.
Even for myself.
My job now,
Is to believe I am safe.
I can tell myself this,
So many times.
But I must show myself now.
I must show myself I am safe.
I have made this safe space.
A safe space for myself.
I can finally breathe.
I finally have room.
Room to believe.
Room to feel safe.

The Final Chapter

This beautiful me.
This me that I have built.
This me, who is here.
Who is here now.
She deserves the best.
She deserves it all.
She deserves to feel safe.
She deserves to be treated well.
She finally believes this.
She has created this.
She has created a world,
Full of love.
She has created a world,
For herself.
She has said her goodbyes.
She will let go of what was,
And what was supposed to be.
She will let go of the possibilities.
She will grieve what she won't have.
She will grieve what she thought would be.
She will give up,
All that she knows.
She will close the book,
On her old life.
She will close that door,
And never look back.
She will grieve and face her pain.
She will face reality.
The end of this chapter.
The final chapter.

The very end of this book.
It is feeling her pain.
It is grieving her life.
It is grieving herself.
It is finding acceptance.
Accepting what was.
Accepting her past.
Finding forgiveness.
The end of this book,
Is opening her heart.
Her heart is fully open.
The very end of this chapter.
It is the end.
Closing this book.
Closing the door.
Ending this pain and opening her heart.

Understood

No one really understands her.
She stands out against the crowd.
She loves solace and quiet.
She loves to be by herself.
She loves to be free,
And not follow the rules.
She does not do well being told what to do.
She listens for her path.
She listens to her intuition.
She listens for her inner guidance.
She follows the signs.
She surrenders herself.
What's meant to be will be.
What is for her will find her.
She completely surrenders.
She gives up all control.
She lets everything go.
She lives in the moment.
She's given up plans.
She lives for right now.
This moment is now.
No one really understands her.
So many try to fix her,
They tell her what to do.
They project their beliefs,
And want her to follow those.
She has her own beliefs,
Separate from anyone else.
She is her own self.
She knows what she needs.

No one really understands her.
She is okay with that.
It took a long time.
A long time to realize.
Realize that she is not here for them.
To be understood,
Is a job for her.
She will learn to understand herself.
It doesn't need to make sense,
To anyone else.
Her path is hers.
Her path is different.
Different than most.
She will keep going,
Not feeling understood.
She will understand herself.
She will hold her confidence,
As she takes her walk.
Walking away from all that she's known.
Letting out every emotion,
That's kept her weighed down.
Letting everything out.
Letting everything go.
Not being understood.
Understood by most.

Who Am I Becoming?

Doing what is best for me.
It will be uncomfortable.
I will feel guilt.
I will feel shame.
I will feel bad,
And that is okay.
People will push back,
When I choose to change.
People will not agree.
Agree with my choice.
This is growth.
This is okay.
I am not made for others.
I am made for me.
I am here,
To learn who I am.
I am here,
To take care of myself.
Please don't feel pressure.
To go back to be that girl.
That girl,
That everyone loves.
That girl,
That everyone wants.
They want that girl back,
But they don't realize she's gone.
Because she has lost,
All that she's had.
She has had to walk away,
From all that she's known.

She is forever changed,
She is not that girl anymore.
I am constantly explaining.
Explaining who I am.
Who I am now,
And no one understands.
The people who have never lost.
The people who have only known love.
The people who don't know betrayal.
These are the people who can't understand.
They don't understand,
Where their girl went.
They want her back,
And she is gone.
I am here now,
Explaining myself.
Surrounded by people,
Who don't know who I am.
They still think I am her.
They can't see me.
They can't see the pain that I have endured.
They can't see all the tears I've cried.
They can't see any of my agony.
I have kept this to myself.
Because I didn't understand.
I didn't even understand,
What was happening to me.
I didn't realize that I had to say goodbye.
Say goodbye to who I was,
In order to be who I am now.
I had to say goodbye,
To all that I was.

Because I lost every part of me,
As I grieved my old life.
Everything I was.
Everything I loved.
It was all attached,
To who I used to be.
To let go of what was,
Is to let go of myself.
Become who I am now.
Become who I was supposed to be.
Find my purpose.
Find my meaning.
Let go of attachment.
Find connection.
Who am I now?
Who am I becoming?

I Am Not The Same

Why is it always my fault?
Why is it always put on me?
Do I carry around a sign,
Saying please put your shit on me?
I am done carrying your shit.
Take your shit back.
This is not mine.
This is yours.
Can you help with the responsibility?
It takes two.
It is not always me.
Please take some accountability.
I am done, always being at fault.
Putting in the work.
Putting in the effort.
Always being the one to make it better.
Always being the one to fix the problem.
I am only one person.
One person,
Who has been through hell.
And still makes room to love you.
And care about your problem.
Care about your shortcomings.
I am the one who listens.
But what about me?
What about my needs?
What about when I need time?
Time to figure out my needs.
Time to figure out my life.
I can't always be there,

For everyone else.
I sometimes need to take care of myself.
I love my people.
I care deeply.
But I need time to feel my feelings.
Figure out why.
Figure out the how's.
Figure out my trauma.
Figure myself out.
I just need some time.
I need my space.
I am not the same.
The same as I was.
My world was ripped out,
From underneath me.
My world that I knew,
Was in shambles.
I had to let it all go.
Everything I loved,
While I watched everyone else,
Building their life up.
My life was crumbling down.
My heart was shattered,
My feelings shoved down.
Shoved away,
So deep down.
I didn't know how to feel any of it.
My heart broken,
My voice was not heard.
What I said,
Didn't matter.
It was all about them.

I became a shell.
A shell of myself.
I kept it all hidden,
Until I didn't.
Until I started speaking up,
Using my voice.
It was time to feel heard.
It was time to explain.
It was time to put myself first,
Finally.
My needs are different.
My needs have changed.
My world collapsed.
I needed to rebuild.
Rebuild myself.
Myself with self-love.
I have found self-love.
Self-love in myself.

Connect With My Body

Connect with myself.
Connect to my body.
I am done disassociating.
It's time to acknowledge.
Acknowledge what I feel.
Acknowledge my feelings.
Acknowledge what is inside.
Inside of me.
Connect with my body.
Connect to myself.
Connect with my feelings.
Connect with my inner knowing.
Where am I carrying my pain?
I feel it in my heart.
Where am I carrying my trauma?
I feel it in my hips.
Where am I carrying my anger?
I feel it in my eyes.
Connect with my body.
This is when I will release.
I am safe now.
I am safe to feel.
I can set my boundaries.
Whatever I need.
It is time to connect.
Connect to my body.
Listen for the sensations.
Physical sensations are here.
Physical problems are emotions,
Manifesting.

Manifesting physically.
The emotions must come out.
My physical pain is telling me.
Sit with my emotions.
There is something to feel.
My body speaks up,
When there is trauma.
The trauma in me,
Must come out.
Anything physical,
I will listen.
Listen closely,
My body will call.
My body is healing.
Calling for freedom.
Calling for release.
Calling for healing.
Listen closely.
Connect with my body.
No more running.
No more disassociation.
My trauma response is here,
To be shut off.
My nervous system calls.
Calls for my attention.
I will listen closely.
Whatever it needs.
Connection is necessary.
I will connect to my body.

Where Did She Go?

"Where is she?"
They say.
"She doesn't come around."
"Where is she?"
"We can't find her."
That's because she's gone.
She has changed.
She is not the same.
She has let everything go.
Everything she knew.
She is not here.
Not anymore.
You will not find her,
Because she is gone.
I know it is hard.
Hard to understand.
Understand where she went,
And understand why.
"Why did she change?"
She carried so much pain,
And it was time to let it go.
It was time for her to become free.
It was time for her,
To put the weight down.
She couldn't go on,
Carrying this pain.
This pain she carried,
For so many years.
This pain she carried.
She carried with her.

All while she,
Cared for everyone else.
She watched everyone build,
While she let everything go.
She always said yes.
She was always there.
She always made an appearance.
She always had a smile on her face.
She was there for everyone's problems.
She was there for everyone's successions.
She was there for every wedding.
She was there when they had their babies.
She was there when they had their traumas.
She was there for everyone else,
While neglecting herself.
Pushing this pain down,
So, she could walk around with a smile.
She walked around being there for everyone else.
All while she sacrificed herself,
And who she was.
It needed to end.
She could no longer do it.
She could not walk around,
Anymore with this pain.
She had to put it down.
She had to feel it.
She had to face her demons,
Without projecting it out.
She didn't want to project.
Project it on anyone else.
This pain was hers.
Hers to face.

No one understood.
Understood what happened.
No one understood.
Understood where she went.
She was constantly explaining.
Explaining why.
Explaining where she went.
Explaining what was happening.
No one understood.
But that is okay.
All she knew,
Was she couldn't carry this pain.
Put it all down.
This weight is not hers.
This weight will not live in her,
Not anymore.
Let it all out.
Let it all go.
Pour everything out.
Detoxify and love.
Love herself,
Like she never has before.
The ones standing at the end,
Are the ones who are meant to be.
Be in her world.
Her new world.
She won't carry a smile,
When she doesn't feel happy.
She won't say she is good,
When she's really burnt out.
She can no longer be there,
For everyone else.

She will be direct.
She will not beat around the bush.
She will take care of herself.
She will learn her needs.
She will no longer agree.
Agree with everything.
She will stop being the people pleaser,
And become her true self.
She will speak her truth.
Her authentic truth.
She will become the girl,
She was always meant to be.
The girl who was put away,
For so many years.
The girl who has been in hiding,
Because she didn't feel safe.
The girl who sacrificed herself,
For everyone else's life.
She was there to give support.
She was there to lift everyone up.
All while her true self,
Was being put aside.
She can't do it anymore.
She deserves so much more.
She deserves to become herself.
Whoever she chooses to be.

The Girl Who No One Gets

I went from the girl who everyone loved,
To being this girl who no one gets.
No one understands.
No one can relate.
I am constantly explaining,
Why I have changed.
I need to walk away.
Walk away from this.
I don't want to be saved.
I don't want to be rescued.
I don't want to be fixed.
I don't want you to have pity.
Have pity on me,
For what I have gone through.
I have been through a lot,
I am aware of this.
The more I heal,
I am triggering others.
Now I watch,
As their trauma responses come out.
They are responding with their egos.
They are responding with their trauma.
The trauma that is inside of them,
Is what they are responding to me with.
No one is aware.
Their eyes are shut.
I need to understand,
This will be my world.
Not everyone will want to live this life.
Live this life,

That I am living.
Eyes wide open,
I see everything.
I see it all,
I don't miss a thing.
Conscious living.
I am awake.
Not everyone wants to face their pain.
Not everyone wants to hear what I have to say.
I am taking these risks.
I am risking myself.
This is how I find my people.
This is how I will find connection.
Take the risk,
Observe what happens.
Put it out there,
And then keep on moving.
Keep going until you are where you need to be.
I don't belong out in this old world,
And that is okay.
I am better here.
I understand myself.
I no longer love being around unawareness.
It is not enjoyable to me.
I am too sensitive to stand it.
Where are my people?
Where are they?
Will anyone ever understand me?
I need someone who gets me.
I need someone who speaks my language.
I need to be understood.
I need to be seen.

Going out into the world,
Everyday.
This is painful,
Having to explain.
I am not who I was.
Do I need to yell it?
I am not that girl,
I used to be.

A Note From The Dr.

"Go on medicine," they said.
You shouldn't be feeling this.
You shouldn't be feeling anything.
You should just feel completely fine.
Just feel happy.
Happy all the time.
Sadness shouldn't come.
Tears shouldn't fall.
You are depressed.
Let us prescribe you a pill.
Life is not difficult,
Emotions should not be felt.
"Go on medicine," they said.
Let us label this.
Label you depressed,
Because you should not feel emotions.
Emotions that are strong.
We don't want to know your past.
We don't need to know what you've been through.
We don't care to put the time in.
We don't care what the root is.
We'll just prescribe you this pill.
An instant quick fix.
This quick fix for your emotions.
Your emotions that have come up.
Life should not be difficult.
Live emotionless.
You should be completely fine.
Stop your crying now,
Put your sadness aside.

Bury it deep down,
Or just take this pill.
Take this antidepressant now,
You will feel completely fine.
You won't have to deal with your emotions,
And neither will we.
We,
The doctors.
You really thought we wanted to deal with emotions?
We,
The doctors.
We don't really care to know.
Know where your emotions stem from.
We just want to prescribe this pill.
Just give this pill.
Label you depressed.
Label you bipolar,
Because you are a mess.
Emotions are looked down on.
Emotions are quickly labeled.
You are given a label,
Along with a pill.
A pill to fix you.
A pill is the quick fix.
Instant gratification,
Is the world we live in.
Prescribe this pill.
Shut your emotions down.
This discomfort that comes,
We have a cure.
This cure,
Known as medicine.

Take this medicine instead of learning.
Learning each emotion.
Learning how to feel.
Learning that these emotions come,
And then they will pass.
Emotions come up,
And then they will leave.
Emotions are not meant to stay.
Take this medicine,
Don't sit with it.
Sit with your emotions?
Why would you do that?
If you show emotion,
You must be mentally sick.
A mental health problem,
Here we go with another label.
If you can't regulate your emotions,
We'll label you bipolar.
Strong emotions,
Need a label.
You're showing sadness?
It is depression.
Sadness that won't go away?
It really must not be your childhood trauma,
You are clinically depressed.
You are addicted to drugs?
But we don't care to know why.
Just treat the main symptom.
You are on drugs,
We'll treat that.
But we won't ever find out why.
Why deep down?

Why are you doing drugs?
We don't really want to know,
Because that takes time.
Too much time.
Time that we don't have.
Time that we won't put in.
But,
Take this pill.
This will fix it.
Quickly,
Let's fix it.
This is what makes us money.
Prescription pills.
Insurance companies.
Hurry,
Just take this pill.
On to the next problem.
We'll label them too.
We don't have time for any of this.
Time for what exactly?
We won't make time to listen or hear you.
We won't make time to get to the root.
We won't make time to get to know you.
Oh, you have a notebook?
Oh, you wrote everything down?
We don't want to hear any of that,
And we don't have time to look.
Hurry, just tell me.
What's going on?
Okay,
Take this pill.
Let's medicate you.

The root cause will have to wait,
Because the more time we spend,
It is money being wasted.
Instant gratification.
This quick fix.
Your emotions,
Turn them down.
Turn them down with this pill.

I Fought Like Hell

I am tired of hiding.
Hiding myself.
I have hid my whole life.
It's time to come out.
Come out with my thoughts.
Come out with my beliefs.
Come out with my story.
This is who I am.
This is me.
I don't need to fit in.
I don't need to be liked.
I don't need to be fixed.
I am just me.
I am not my old self.
The one who used to hide.
Hide who I am,
Because I wanted to be liked.
The one who use to hide,
And minimized myself.
Minimized everything.
Minimized was my thing.
My shit doesn't matter,
So let me push it down.
Hide it away,
So, no one can see.
I hid who I was,
For so many years.
I hid what I went through,
Because I was loyal.
I hid what I went through.

I did it for love.
I did it for protection.
I did it out of fear.
I am done with that life.
I don't care anymore.
I am not responsible for your feelings.
I am not responsible for you.
I am responsible for me,
And that is it.
I am this girl,
I have fought so hard for.
I have fought like hell.
To be where I am.
I fought like hell,
To let everything go.
I have fought like hell,
To heal myself.
I have fought like hell,
To be where I am.
I have fought like hell,
For myself.
Why hide her now?
After fighting like hell.
I have been treated like shit.
I have been walked on and stomped on.
I have been talked down to and abused.
And I am done with all of that.
I have the biggest heart.
A heart of gold.
I won't let anyone break it.
Not ever again.
I have a heart of gold,

That has been shattered.
I have a heart of gold,
That has been stomped on.
I am done being abused.
I am done being used.
I am done being manipulated.
I am done being misunderstood.
I am done hiding all of this.
It is what it is.
It is in my past now.
I am not going to hide myself.
This is my gift.
This is my gift,
I am giving to myself.
I will say what I have to say.
I will be who I want to be.
I will do what I have to do.
I am just ready to be me.
I am not going to hide,
Not anymore.
This is who I am now,
And you don't have to stay.
I am used to people leaving,
That has been my life.
I want you to be here,
But only if you want to be.
I have let everything go.
I have said my goodbyes.
If you don't like me,
That is fine.
I bent over backwards,
Trying to be liked.

I sacrificed myself,
Just to fit in.
The people pleaser,
Yes, that was me.
Make everyone happy,
Put myself last.
I hid who I was,
So, I could have a place.
Have a place in everyone else's life,
Like mine didn't matter.
My life matters.
I have realized,
I matter.
I can be whoever I want to be.
I will not stay where I have always stayed.
Everything changes,
That is constant.
I will accept this,
And stop hiding who I am.

Time For Me To Change Now

Do I need to explain?
Keep explaining?
Why is everyone bent out of shape,
Because I am changing?
Isn't that life?
To change and to grow.
Life doesn't stay the same,
It is constantly moving.
We are not made to stay in one spot.
We are not made to be the same person.
We are not made to please everyone else.
I am allowed to change.
I can decide my path.
Why do I need to explain?
Explain where I went.
Can't everyone see?
Why I would change.
My life fell apart.
My world collapsed.
Who would stay the same,
After that?
I have sat for many years,
Watching everyone in my world change.
I have sat and watched everyone else build up their life.
I sat and supported.
I sat and cheered everyone on.
I was the cheerleader.
I was the lifter.
I was their number one supporter.
Supporter of change.

Supporter of growth.
I have always supported everyone's happiness.
I have listened to the cries,
I have helped to wipe many tears.
But the minute,
I change.
The minute,
I am different.
I get push back,
No one understands.
My needs are important.
I am important.
My voice is important.
My life is important.
I have looked back to see,
How much of myself I gave away.
Never taking the time,
To figure out who I am.
Never taking the time,
To hear my inner voice.
Never taking the time,
To follow my heart.
It is my time now.
It is my turn now.
Time for me to change now.

Right Now

This path I chose.
This path of now.
This journey I will enjoy.
This journey is mine.
The journey with no end,
No destination.
There is no outcome.
No expectation.
The path can change,
At any time.
There is no plan,
Let go of that.
Just trust in now.
Trust in right now.
Let go of control,
There is no such thing.
Control what happens,
I can't do that.
Control the expectation,
I can't do that.
Control the outcome,
I can't do that.
The only thing I have control over is me.
My reaction.
My response.
Let it all go,
Set my ego free.
Erasing the big picture.
Focus on just one step.
This step,

Right now.
That's where I am at.
This is my focus.
Dropping the control.
Dropping the big picture.
Dropping my ego.
All that matters,
Is this moment.
This moment,
Right now.
Letting go of the outcome.

I Needed Rest

All I needed.
Needed was rest.
Rest from running.
Running from myself.
Always running.
Always distracting.
All I needed.
I needed rest.
Rest for myself.
Rest for my heart.
Rest for my inner child.
My inner child,
Who was hurt.
She was hurting for so many years.
And all I did was run.
Anything to distract.
Distract from myself.
My inner child needed me,
And all I did was run.
I have stopped this behavior.
I have stopped doing this.
I have stopped running.
I have stopped my distractions.
Addicted to running.
Addicted to numbing.
Put a smile on my face,
And just keep going.
Never stopping.
Never resting.
All I needed was rest,

And I didn't pay attention.
I was not accepted,
If I had emotions.
God forbid I feel,
Without a smile on my face.
To rest,
Is to stop.
And I didn't know how.
I didn't know how to stop,
Until I figured it out.
I figured myself out,
When I started to rest.
Rest and slow down.
I don't have to have it all figured out.
All I need now,
Is to rest.

Piece By Piece

I made this life.
This life for myself.
This life is peaceful.
This life is safe.
I have done well.
Done well for myself.
I figured it out,
Pretty much by myself.
I followed my gut.
I listened to my heart.
A lot of healing.
A lot of trusting.
Trusting in myself.
I surrendered it all.
Let go of my life.
Let go of the world.
The world that I knew.
This is not for me,
I must keep going.
Gather the pieces.
The pieces of myself.
The pieces that broke,
Gather them up.
I will pick up each piece.
I will repair myself.
Picking up each piece,
And making myself whole.
Piece by piece,
It all comes together.
Piece by piece,

I become whole.
Piece by piece,
This process is mine.
Piece by piece,
I will not leave any behind.
Piece by piece,
I feel this pain.
Piece by piece,
Each piece of myself.
Each piece has a story.
I will listen closely.
Piece by piece,
I will pay attention.
Each piece I pick up,
I learn who I am.
Each piece I pick up,
Gives me my worth.
Each piece I pick up,
The illusion falls off.
Each piece I pick up,
I see so clearly.
Each piece I pick up,
This creates my mirror.
A mirror I will look in,
To see myself.
At the end of this process,
I will hold up this mirror.
This mirror of all the pieces.
The pieces I have picked up.
This mirror is cracked.
This mirror is not perfect.
This mirror I look in,

Each piece of myself.
This mirror is made up of,
Each piece I have picked up.
I see each piece,
That makes this whole.
This whole mirror.
This mirror is flawed.
I love each piece.
I love each flaw.
I love each line.
I love each crack.
This whole mirror,
That I look in.
I will look in everyday,
And appreciate each piece.

Walking Away From Where You Came From

Walking away from where you came from,
It is the hardest thing you will do.
Walking away from where you came from,
It leaves this huge void in your heart.
It will bring grief,
Like you have never felt before.
It is a pain,
Like you have never felt before.
This is not a decision that comes overnight.
This is not a decision that you make just one time.
It is a choice,
A boundary that comes.
A boundary that comes to set you free.
The only boundary you can have,
To be able to be who you are supposed to be.
The only boundary that works,
For you to feel completely safe.
But this choice comes with a price.
A price that you pay.
An emotional price.
These emotions you will feel,
Are like you've never felt before.
These emotions you will feel,
Will knock you completely down.
These emotions you will feel,
Are so intense.
So intense,
You can't stand up.
So intense,
You can't even breathe.

So intense,
You really can't function.
But once you let yourself feel them,
You set yourself free.
Free from a life,
That held you back.
Free from a life,
That weighed you down.
Free from a life,
Where you couldn't be yourself.
Free from a life,
Where you had to become someone else.
Free from a life,
Where you had to wear a mask.
Free from a life,
That kept you from your path.
Free from a life,
With extreme emotional abuse.
Free from a life,
Where you were used.
Free from a life,
Where you weren't seen.
Free from a life,
Where you were an extension of them.
You will be free.
Free from this world.
This world of betrayal.
This world of self-sacrifice.
This world kept you from your heart.
This world kept you from your soul.
The only way back.
The only way back to yourself,

Is to walk away from this world.
The only world you ever knew.
Walking away from where you came from,
Is not just one choice.
It is a million days of misery.
A million days of agony.
A million days of grief.
Walking away from the only love you knew,
Is the hardest decision you will ever make.
It is the only way to your true self.
Walking away from where you came from,
There were a million reasons why.
A million reasons that added up,
To know that walking away was right.
This decision,
Is ending your life.
Ending your life,
Ending that girl.
That girl.
That role.
The daughter.
A girl with a family.
Ending these labels.
Ending these roles.
Walking into the unknown,
Not knowing where to go.
Not knowing how to function,
Without being part of something.
Embracing the unknown,
And falling in love with the process.
Embracing the present moment,
Becomes what you trust.

Living in a world,
Where you finally feel safe.
You finally feel safe.
You can finally breathe.
Walking away from where you came from,
Brings more grief you will ever feel.
So why even do it?
Why go through this misery?
Why go through this agonizing pain?
Because, at the end.
At the end of this journey,
You will find a freedom,
You never knew existed.
You will find a freedom,
You have never felt before.
You will find a safety,
You have never even known.
And the biggest reward,
Is to be the girl you were always supposed to be.
The biggest reward,
Is you are in touch with your soul.
Your soul,
That just couldn't ever survive in that world.
The biggest reward is that you will fulfil your dreams.
Your dreams,
That you couldn't fulfil,
While you were playing that role.

Loss

Loss will change you.
Loss is an introduction,
To a pathway that you've never experienced before.
Loss will guide you,
Into emotions that are completely debilitating.
Loss brings you to a shift.
You will feel unequipped.
How do I handle this?
How do I live?
Loss brings you to an awakening.
Everything is different.
Nothing is the same.
A void in your heart.
Most people will not understand.
Loss takes away your life,
Of how it was before.
Your life,
It looks so different now.
Loss changes your heart.
Your life after loss,
You will change.
Your heart will change.
You will never be the same.
Loss and love have a connection.
Because without love,
There would be no loss.
The loss wouldn't matter.
The loss wouldn't have an effect.
The loss could be shrugged off.
Just move on.
But with love and loss,

It leaves a hole.
It leaves a void.
That love has nowhere to go.
Loss brings grief.
Grief brings waves.
Waves that you drown in.
Waves that you just can't explain.
Grief becomes a part of you,
That you carry with you every day.
Grief is forever,
It really does not leave.
It's how you begin to carry it.
Carry these waves,
Alongside you in life.
These waves are now,
A part of you.
Your grief and my grief,
May not look the same.
The waves may come at different times,
Different speeds.
Your wave may be foggy,
Mine may be turbulent.
Your wave may be calm,
Mine may be heavy.
Loss without love wouldn't be a burden.
But I love with all that I have,
So my loss will feel heavy.
Your loss and my loss
May feel different.
But loss is loss.
And
Love is love.

This Grip

This fear.
You are gripping.
Gripping onto parts of you.
Parts of you that you don't want to lose.
Parts of you that everyone loved.
Parts of you that everyone saw.
Parts of you that everyone knows.
Parts of you that you don't want to lose.
You are gripping.
Gripping so tight.
Almost too tight,
It's okay to let go.
What is your fear?
This fear you have.
It keeps coming back.
It keeps coming up.
A fear that you are leaving behind.
Leaving behind,
Parts of you.
Once again,
More to lose.
How much more can you lose?
Gripping so tight.
Too tight to let go.
Your journey is not to hold on too tight.
That was old.
Old parts of you.
Old parts of you that wanted to be loved.
This fear you have,
It is okay to feel it.

Acknowledge it,
Feel it,
Then release it.
Release and let go.
Let go of this.
It's okay to let go.
Release this grip.
Gripping so tight,
The further you go.
The further and further away you get.
The further away,
From your old life.
The further away,
From your old self.
The further away society feels.
The further away everyone feels.
Deeper and deeper inside of yourself.
This fear you have,
Let it go.
Release your grip.
This grip you have.
This grip you have on parts of you.
Parts of you that you no longer need.
Parts of you that are holding you back.
Holding you back,
From your true self.
Gripping for external love.
Gripping for external acceptance.
This isn't needed.
Not anymore.
This grip you have,
Release this hold.

Holding onto these old parts.
These old parts, that weigh you down.
This grip you have,
It is more to lose.
Let it go,
You are here to lose.
Lose it all,
Let it go.
Lose it all,
To become who you are.

This Fearful Girl

This fearful girl.
She is here.
She is here to tell you she's scared.
She is here because she feels fear.
She feels fear because she has given up control.
She has given up her path,
Of knowing what's next.
She has given up wanting a final outcome.
She is walking into the unknown.
An unknown,
That she doesn't know.
She doesn't know which way to go.
She doesn't know how to navigate.
She doesn't know what is next.
This scares her,
This unknown.
She never appreciated change before.
She didn't like change,
She wanted to know.
She wanted to know where she was headed.
She wanted to know her next step.
She wanted to have an expectation.
She didn't have trust.
She didn't have faith.
She just had control,
And that was all she knew.
This fearful girl,
Did not go to the unknown.
She needed to know.
She now has learned that is not how life works.

She has learned these lessons,
That life is not known.
Life can't be predicted.
Life will change.
Change is constant.
She will detach from the outcome.
Because she expects a certain outcome,
This is where she finds disappointment.
Disappointment and let downs,
And she can't control it.
She will let go of this vision.
She will let go of expectations.
She will let go of her control,
As she walks into the unknown.
Unknown territory,
Is where she will go.
Fear lives in the unknown.
Most people like certainty,
Where they can control.
To give up any certainty,
Is to feel fear.
It is learning to walk with this fear,
Side by side.
Side by side into the unknown.
There is no outcome in the unknown.
There is no plan.
There is no certainty.
Anything can happen,
Anything goes.
Words can be said,
That people don't like.
People will change,

Situations will go awry.
This fearful girl will now accept.
Accept her life in this unknown.
Looking back,
Into her old life.
She was constantly filled with disappointment.
Disappointment that she could not control.
This fearful girl,
I have brought her along.
Along into this new world.
Showing her how the unknown is safe.
The unknown is okay,
We feel better this way.
This fearful girl,
It's okay to let go.
It's okay to detach,
And release this fear.
Her old world was so black and white.
She knew what was ahead.
She knew what to expect.
People pleasing was her way,
Dropping everything for her friends.
Saying what everyone wants to hear.
Playing a role that wasn't her,
Just so she could feel safe and loved.
She found her worth in the unknown.
This fearful girl will slowly see.
See that life is okay.
See that life doesn't need to be known.
Enjoy each moment as it comes.
Enjoy each step.
Each step she takes.

Projection

I say something,
And you say something back.
Projecting your opinion.
Projecting how you feel,
About the topic.
Projecting your beliefs.
Projecting how you feel,
All while putting me down.
I know you don't mean it.
I know you aren't aware.
Aware that you are projecting how you feel.
How you feel,
Onto me.
I am my own person.
I have my own beliefs.
I have my own feelings,
I don't need yours to bleed onto me.
This realization that I have come to,
Makes interactions so much better.
Your response to what I am saying,
Has more to do with you.
Projecting your thought process.
Your beliefs are not mine.
I am not going to agree,
With your projection you have put on me.
You have your opinion.
I have my own too.
What you think,
Is not what I think.

I am my own person,
I know what I need.
I don't need you to project onto me.

Fear Of The Unknown

She fears the unknown.
Let it be.
She fears uncertainty.
Let it go.
She fears something will happen.
What if this.
What if that.
Must always have a plan.
Must always know.
Know the end.
Know another choice.
Another choice if her plan doesn't work.
Always have a backup plan.
Always know,
Always prepare.
Prepare with control.
Control the outcome.
Control the plan.
Control what happens in the end.
This is a lesson,
She must learn.
She must learn,
To love again.
She must learn,
To find herself.
Find herself in the unknown.
Trust herself,
Without control.
Trust herself,
Without the plan.

Trust herself.
Trust in the unknown.
Trust her heart,
To find where she'll end up.
Painting a picture,
Of what she wants.
Letting go of her life,
The one she built.
She built this life,
With her pain.
Letting go of her pain.
Letting of her control.
She finds herself,
With a new goal.
She finds herself,
Being okay.
Being okay with the unknown.
Sit in the stillness.
Get rid of the noise.
All she's left with,
Is herself.
All she hears,
Is her pain.
She will hear it.
She will honor it,
And then she will release it.
With each release,
She feels safer.
She finds herself feeling,
Safe in the unknown.

Inside Stillness

Everyday,
She wakes up.
She wakes up without a plan.
Everyday,
She wakes up.
She wakes up seeing how she feels.
Everyday,
She will say.
Say to herself,
"What will today bring?"
Today is unknown,
And so is tomorrow.
She will move,
Moment to moment.
Whatever the moment brings,
Is what she will do.
She will live.
Live her life like this.
She will open her eyes,
Each morning.
Each morning,
Not knowing.
Not knowing what comes next.
She doesn't know what is in store.
What is in store for her future.
And she is okay with that.
There is no rush.
There is no pressure.
There is no decision that needs to be made.
This is her gift.

She will give to the world.
Just be present.
Just be here.
Just be in this moment.
Nothing is definite.
Nothing is exact.
And what is meant to be,
Will be.
She loves to sit.
Sit in stillness.
Inside stillness,
Is where the present moment resides.
She loves to listen.
Listen to quiet.
She loves to feel.
Feel her breath.
Her breath will tell her what is next.
She listens for signals.
She listens for signs.
She listens for her inner guidance.
This is only heard,
Inside of stillness.

She Has Earned Her Right

She has earned her right.
Her right to her voice.
She has earned her right.
Her right to her thoughts.
She has earned her right.
Her right to her beliefs.
She will use her voice,
When she needs.
She will stand by,
What is right.
What is right for her,
She will fight for.
She will no longer allow herself.
Allow herself to be walked on.
She will no longer allow herself.
Allow herself to feel neglected.
She knows what she needs.
She will figure it out.
She will listen to herself,
She has earned this right.

The Illusion Is Really Gone Now

The illusion wore off.
This illusion is gone.
This lens I knew,
This lens was fogged.
This lens I saw through,
This lens was not real.
This illusion I knew.
This illusion was my life.
This illusion I saw.
I saw with my trauma.
My lens was fogged with my pain.
This illusion I knew,
I thought was real.
I did not even realize,
This was my trauma.
So naïve.
This illusion of denial.
Living in this distortion,
With a smile on my face.
Living like this,
For so many years.
How did I not see this?
This illusion is gone.
I sit here now,
In real life.
In real life,
Without a lens.
What a shocker,
Without the illusion.
Unbelievable,

Oh my god.
Wow,
I see clearly now.
I've reached so deeply in myself now,
I see it so clearly now.
Feel it all now.
This illusion of the world,
It is gone now.
It is just me now,
Seeing it all now.
It is clear now.
The illusion is really gone now.

To Rise Is To Fall

Build it up,
To let it go.
Build it higher,
To have it fall.
You must rise,
Then you will fall.
You must come up,
To fall to the ground.
Build it up.
Let it fall.
Create it,
For it to collapse.
Let it all go.
It is weighing you down.
Feel it leave,
As you let it go.
Walk away,
One final time.
Keep on walking,
As you let it fall.
Fall out of you.
Put this weight down.
You won't carry it anymore.
Drop it,
It's not yours.
Build it up.
Let it go.
Climb the stairs,
To fall all the way down.
Crash to the bottom.

Lay there at the bottom.
Looking to the top.
Wondering how to get back up.
Way up there.
Stay down here.
The tools are down here.
It's okay to be down here.
The lessons are down here.
Surrender is down here.
Surrender it all.
Let it all go,
Down here.
To rise is to fall.
To fall,
Is to get back up.

Grief Will Change You

Grief will change you.
You will never be the same.
Giving up your heart,
To grieve what you loved.
Grieving yourself,
And all that you loved.
All that you loved,
Filled up your heart.
Love will change you,
But so will grief.
Loss tears you apart.
Loss changes who you are.
Loss gives life a whole new meaning.
Grieving yourself.
Grieving those parts.
Love will change you,
But so will grief.
Grieving what you loved.
Pieces of your heart,
Taken away.
Visions you saw,
Is part of grief.
Painting a picture of what you want,
Just to lose it.
Lose it all.
Growth is grieving.
Growth may mean leaving.
Leaving all that you know,
To get to where you will end up.
Grieving that life.

Grieving that world.
Grieving betrayal.
Grieving the illusion.
Love will change you,
But so will loss.
Grief will change you,
And so will pain.
Your heart will never, ever be the same.

Once You See, You Cannot Unsee

You won't see,
Until you are ready to see.
So much to see,
But until you are ready...
You just won't see it.
See the big picture.
See reality.
See what is going on,
What is really happening.
You will only see the illusion.
The illusion you put on.
Put on for safety.
Your armor.
Your guard.
You won't see,
Until you are ready to see.
And once you do see,
You cannot unsee.
Take down the armor.
The illusion falls.
Here you are,
Without the fog.
Without the walls.
That illusion,
You thought.
You thought was real.
You have to be ready.
You have to have the tools.
You have to have the space.
The space to hold.

The space to hold reality.
Hold this reality without the fear.
It's okay,
You are safe.
You are safe now,
Without this lens.
This is reality.
This is real.
It's okay to see,
You are ready now.
You are leaving denial.
You are leaving the illusion.
This illusion came from society.
This illusion came from your upbringing.
This illusion was passed down,
From generation to generation.
It is now time to break this generational curse.
It is your turn now,
To live how you want.
Live without this illusion,
That you have been living behind.
Without this illusion,
You become free.
These rose-colored glasses are no longer yours.
Put them down.
It's time to see.
Time to see,
Without them on.
It's time to see,
What is real.
And once you see,
You cannot unsee.

This will stay with you,
What is real.
You have to be strong enough.
Strong enough to see.
You have to be ready.
Ready to see.
And once you see,
You cannot unsee.

I Feel It Deep Inside

It's time for me to go now.
It's time for me to leave.
I am burnt out,
Burnt out from this life I live.
It's time for a new chapter.
A new chapter.
A new life.
Live for me now.
Go where I want now.
Go where my soul belongs now.
It's time for me to go now.
Leave this life I lived.
Leave this place I've been in,
My whole life.
It used to mean the world to me.
It used to fill my heart.
It used to be my home.
It used to be my love.
I don't belong here anymore.
I feel it dep inside.
I feel it every day as soon as I open my eyes.
I feel it all day long.
I feel it every night.
This voice I hear.
It gets louder each day.
I don't belong here anymore.
I feel it deep inside.
I have disconnected from this life.
This life that I have lived.
My heart was here,

And now it's not.
I listen for this voice.
This voice is my soul.
Calling me.
Calling me to leave.
"This life is not for you,
It's time for you to leave now."
I hear this every single day.
I feel it in my heart.
Knowing that I just can't stay.
Stay for everyone else,
Is the hardest part.
I must choose me.
Choose what is best.
Choose to go,
Where I'm supposed to be.
Sure, I'm scared.
There is that fear.
But I know, on the other side.
The other side of fear,
Lives a life that is waiting for me.
This life is waiting.
This life that is calling.
This is my soul speaking.
This voice, I hear.
I must go to where I am aligned.
I must let everything go.
Everything I knew and everything I had.
This is my destiny,
I feel it deep inside.

The End

The end of me.
The old me,
Who everyone knows.
The end of that girl.
My old life,
It no longer aligns.
Aligns with who I want to be.
Aligns with where I want to be.
Aligns with my soul.
Aligns with my needs.
This doesn't serve me anymore.
Keep moving.
Keep going.
This doesn't fit.
This doesn't work.
It is the end.
The end of me.
That old me,
Who everyone loved.
The girl who makes everyone happy.
The girl who cannot disappoint.
Taking on everyone's problems,
Just to be loved.
All while doing it,
With a smile on her face.
I am done.
The end.
The end of all that.
I need to find what I love.
Walk away from this life.

It is the end.
The end of sacrificing myself.
The end of going out of my way.
The end of fixing everything.
The end of pleasing everyone.
Everyone,
Other than myself.
The end.
Goodbye.
I have to go.
I can't live one more day,
As that girl.
Words will come out,
That they don't want to hear.
Honest.
Truthful.
The words that align with me.
Words are spoken.
Direct,
To the point.
I won't be sugarcoating,
Not anymore.
It is what it is.
This is who I am.
No more hiding.
The end.

The Shadow Of You

My dreams couldn't come true,
While I was still there.
Still entertaining your needs,
My dreams I could not see.
Until I walked away.
My dreams are coming true.
Now in the shadow.
The shadow of you.
I am leaving this shadow.
And the further away I get,
The clearer I see.
The clearer my dreams become.
Clarity is coming,
In the shadows of you.
The further the shadow,
The less weight I carry.
The lighter I become on this journey.
The less foggy my path is.
The stormy weather is gone.
These barricades are moving.
There is nothing in my way.
I am standing in the shadows.
The shadows of you.
My tears are streaming.
They keep falling.
The grief is heavy.
But time will heal.
Your shadow I see.
The effects of you are lurking.
Traumatized still,

But healing is here.
I found healing in the shadows of you.
I found my dreams in the shadows of you.
The more I heal,
The further I walk.
Further and further from the shadow of you.
I am looking back now at the shadow of you.
And all I see now,
Are all of my dreams coming true.

They Couldn't See Themselves

They couldn't see themselves,
So, they could not see her.
They could not see her,
Properly.
They saw her,
Through their own lens.
They used her for their own needs,
To fill a void.
A void in them,
That they could not see.
They will keep on using her for their needs.
They will keep dumping on her,
As they please.
Because they can.
Because she allows it.
She doesn't speak up.
She doesn't set boundaries.
It is all about them.
All about their needs,
And never about hers.
The day she speaks up,
Is when they will leave.
She is no good to them anymore.
She can't be used,
She figured them out.
She is not filling their void.
They will move on.
Get their needs met by someone else.
Someone who can't see,
That this is going on.

Someone who is not aware.
Aware of this game.
Someone who is naïve,
Like she used to be.
They can no longer take,
Advantage of her kindness.
Because she is now protected.
Protected from them.
She has now accepted...
That none of this behavior,
Has anything to do with her.
These are their problems to figure out,
She is not here to fix them.
This is their void to deal with,
This is not hers.
Why is she taking this on,
It is her turn now.
They cannot see themselves,
So how can they see her?
She has decided she is done with transactions.
Transactional love.
Love with conditions.
She will love unconditionally,
And find the others who love the same way as her.

Forgiveness

I forgive you.
I forgive me.
I forgive,
This insanity.
I forgive,
This chaos.
I forgive,
The illusion.
I forgive it all.
This will be the conclusion.
Forgiveness is hard to find.
First, I had to see it all.
Forgiveness is a process,
It's not just one act.
First, I had to understand.
I had to find compassion.
I had to move through,
A lot of anger.
I had to cry,
Many tears.
As I moved through all of these emotions,
I finally felt safe in my own body.
I gave myself,
Everything I needed.
I gave myself,
Everything I asked for.
I listened intensely,
To every signal.
I rested.
And sat in complete stillness.

As I moved through all of this,
I started to find forgiveness.
Forgiveness for myself.
Forgiveness for everyone else.
Within this forgiveness,
Was acceptance.
I accept all of this.
I am no longer the victim.
Once I could forgive,
I started to be thankful.
That all of this came as a lesson.
The chaos.
The fire.
It was all a lesson.
I forgive you.
I forgive me.
I forgive it all.
Forgiveness sets you free.

Life's Journey

Let go of those expectations.
Let go of the pressure.
Let go of false beliefs.
Let go of separation.
Let go of black and white.
Let go of putting up a façade.
Let go of your mask.
Let go your old world,
It's okay.
Moving on,
It is hard.
Acceptance,
Is even harder.
Everything changes,
Let it all go.
Accepting that it is different.
Different than how you wanted it to turn out.
Live for the moment,
Because the future is not known.
The future cannot be controlled.
Controlled by you.
Live for this moment,
Because this is where you are.
You are here now,
Letting it all go.
It doesn't feel good.
It feels so lonely.
It feels like there is no end,
And that is okay.
There's nothing to fix.

There's nothing to do.
Somethings aren't meant to make sense,
Somethings are meant to just accept.
Accept that this is how life turned out.
Accept that this is where you are.
Putting it all down,
Letting it all go...
Leaves you feeling,
Empty and hurt.
This is all okay,
This is part of life.
This is life's journey.

Where you Belong

When you are not in alignment.
Alignment with your soul.
Your body tells you.
Listen for the signals.
The signals will tell you.
Every day when you wake up.
Every time you go out.
Any conversation you have...
It is there,
In the back of your mind.
This voice,
Gets louder and louder the longer you wait.
Day by day,
The louder this voice gets.
This voice will start screaming,
If you choose to stay.
Stay where you are.
Stay where you have always been.
Stay where you don't belong.
Stay where you don't fit.
This voice will scream.
It will not just leave.
This voice lives deep.
Deep within you.
This voice is your soul,
Calling you.
This voice might not make sense.
The big picture is not there yet.
Take it small step by small step...
One detail at a time.

It might not make sense to you yet,
But your soul knows.
Your soul knows you better,
Than anyone else.
Life cannot be planned out,
That has been proven.
Let go of the plan.
Let go of the future.
Trust in right now.
Trust in these signals.
Trust in this deep knowing.
This knowing in you.
Your heart will tell you,
When it is time.
When it is time,
To leave things behind.
This voice.
These signals.
Trust in them.
You will trust in yourself,
More than you ever have.
Your soul is in charge now.
Let it lead the way.
Let go of control.
Let go of perfection.
Let go of the plan.
Trust in your heart.
Leave where you are,
To go where you belong.

She Will Fly Free

Her hair in the wind.
Her windows down.
She feels like she can fly.
Fly with the wind.
Wherever the wind blows,
She will go.
Wherever she ends up,
Is where she will be.
The wind will take her,
She is free.
Bring love to the world,
As she heals.
She brings freedom and light,
Wherever she goes.
Her hair, blowing in the wind.
She has wings.
Wings she has earned,
By crying many tears.
Wings she put on,
After facing her fears.
Sitting with herself.
In her cocoon.
She grew her wings.
These wings will carry her,
Wherever she ends up.
These wings are hers.
A sign of her love.
Love for herself.
She will fly free.

Thank you.
Sending you hope.

I dedicate this book to all of you doing the work
to find your true, authentic selves.